Current
CONTROVERSIES

| Racism

DISCARD

Other Books in the Current Controversies series

Racism

Noël Merino, Book Editor

GREENHAVEN PRESS
A part of Gale, Cengage Learning

Detroit • New York • San Francisco • New Haven, Conn • Waterville, Maine • London

Christine Nasso, *Publisher*
Elizabeth Des Chenes, *Managing Editor*

© 2009 Greenhaven Press, a part of Gale, Cengage Learning

For more information, contact:
Greenhaven Press
27500 Drake Rd.
Farmington Hills, MI 48331-3535
Or you can visit our Internet site at gale.cengage.com

For product information and technology assistance, contact us at

Gale Customer Support, 1-800-877-4253
For permission to use material from this text or product, submit all requests online at www.cengage.com/permissions

Further permissions questions can be emailed to permissionrequest@cengage.com

Articles in Greenhaven Press anthologies are often edited for length to meet page requirements. In addition, original titles of these works are changed to clearly present the main thesis and to explicitly indicate the author's opinion. Every effort is made to ensure that Greenhaven Press accurately reflects the original intent of the authors. Every effort has been made to trace the owners of copyrighted material.

Cover image © Catherine Ivill/AMA/Corbis.

LIBRARY OF CONGRESS CATALOGING-IN-PUBLICATION DATA

Racism / Noël Merino, book editor.
   p. cm. -- (Current controversies)
   Includes bibliographical references and index.
   ISBN-13: 978-0-7377-4462-0 (hardcover)
   ISBN-13: 978-0-7377-4463-7 (pbk.)
   1. Racism--United States. 2. United States--Race relations. I. Merino, Noël.
   E185.615.R2147 2009
   305.800973--dc22
                                                              2009012037

Printed in the United States of America
1 2 3 4 5 6 7 13 12 11 10 09

Contents

Chapter 4: What Should Be Done About Racism?

Foreword

By definition, controversies are "discussions of questions in which opposing opinions clash" (*Webster's Twentieth Century Dictionary Unabridged*). Few would deny that controversies are a pervasive part of the human condition and exist on virtually every level of human enterprise. Controversies transpire between individuals and among groups, within nations and between nations. Controversies supply the grist necessary for progress by providing challenges and challengers to the status quo. They also create atmospheres where strife and warfare can flourish. A world without controversies would be a peaceful world; but it also would be, by and large, static and prosaic.

The Series' Purpose

The purpose of the *Current Controversies* series is to explore many of the social, political, and economic controversies dominating the national and international scenes today. Titles selected for inclusion in the series are highly focused and specific. For example, from the larger category of criminal justice, *Current Controversies* deals with specific topics such as police brutality, gun control, white collar crime, and others. The debates in *Current Controversies* also are presented in a useful, timeless fashion. Articles and book excerpts included in each title are selected if they contribute valuable, long-range ideas to the overall debate. And wherever possible, current information is enhanced with historical documents and other relevant materials. Thus, while individual titles are current in focus, every effort is made to ensure that they will not become quickly outdated. Books in the *Current Controversies* series will remain important resources for librarians, teachers, and students for many years.

In addition to keeping the titles focused and specific, great care is taken in the editorial format of each book in the series. Book introductions and chapter prefaces are offered to provide background material for readers. Chapters are organized around several key questions that are answered with diverse opinions representing all points on the political spectrum. Materials in each chapter include opinions in which authors clearly disagree as well as alternative opinions in which authors may agree on a broader issue but disagree on the possible solutions. In this way, the content of each volume in *Current Controversies* mirrors the mosaic of opinions encountered in society. Readers will quickly realize that there are many viable answers to these complex issues. By questioning each author's conclusions, students and casual readers can begin to develop the critical thinking skills so important to evaluating opinionated material.

Current Controversies is also ideal for controlled research. Each anthology in the series is composed of primary sources taken from a wide gamut of informational categories including periodicals, newspapers, books, U.S. and foreign government documents, and the publications of private and public organizations. Readers will find factual support for reports, debates, and research papers covering all areas of important issues. In addition, an annotated table of contents, an index, a book and periodical bibliography, and a list of organizations to contact are included in each book to expedite further research.

Perhaps more than ever before in history, people are confronted with diverse and contradictory information. During the Persian Gulf War, for example, the public was not only treated to minute-to-minute coverage of the war, it was also inundated with critiques of the coverage and countless analyses of the factors motivating U.S. involvement. Being able to sort through the plethora of opinions accompanying today's major issues, and to draw one's own conclusions, can be a complicated and frustrating struggle. It is the editors' hope that *Current Controversies* will help readers with this struggle.

Introduction

> *"The extent of the problem of racism for African Americans in contemporary society is a topic of heated debate, especially given the election of Barack Obama, the first African American president of the United States."*

Racism is the discrimination or prejudice toward a group of people because of their race. Race itself is a challenging concept to define. The average person on the street most likely makes determinations about race based on skin color, facial features, and hair. Whether or not there are important differences among people beneath this level of appearance is open to debate. On one side are people such as scientist C. Loring Brace, who claims that "there is no such thing as a biological entity that warrants the term 'race.'"[1] On the other side are people who claim that there are important genetic differences among races—Richard J. Herrnstein and Charles Murray argued in their controversial 1994 book *The Bell Curve* that race leads to differences in intelligence. Even if there is acknowledgment that differences exist between races, however, such differences do not warrant racism, which typically involves assertions that one group is superior to another. Whether or not race is a meaningful concept, there is no doubt that racism exists in people's *beliefs* about the significance of race.

The United States has a history that is blighted by acts of racism toward different groups. Since the arrival of European settlers, Native Americans have been subject to racial discrimination. African Americans became a notable target of racism, beginning with slavery and extending far beyond. During World War II, thousands of Japanese Americans were confined in internment camps throughout the West, their patriotism and loyalty questioned because of their race. Mexican Americans, subject to racism in the United States for more than a century, have been a renewed target in recent decades as the dialogue about immigration reaches a fever pitch.

Although many kinds of racism exist in the United States, perhaps none is so recognizable or prevalent throughout American history as the racism regarding African Americans. According to the U.S. Census Bureau, African Americans are the single largest racial minority in the United States (though the U.S. Census does not categorize Latinos as a distinct race). What is unique about African Americans as a group is how they came to the United States: Most African Americans are descendents of Africans forcibly brought to North America, between the seventeenth and nineteenth centuries, to be slaves. At the height of slavery, in 1860, according to the U.S. Census Bureau, there were almost four million black slaves in the United States. In 1865, after the end of the Civil War, the Thirteenth Amendment to the U.S. Constitution was adopted, officially abolishing slavery. Nonetheless, the legacy of slavery left its mark on race relations between whites and blacks, and African Americans continued to suffer from racism in the United States.

In the late 1890s, southern states enacted laws known as Jim Crow laws, which enforced racial segregation in all aspects of African Americans' lives: where they lived, where they went to school, where they worked, how they traveled. The constitutionality of these laws was upheld by the U.S. Supreme Court in 1896 with the *Plessy v. Ferguson* decision. It was not until the civil rights movement of the 1950s and 1960s that such laws were finally eliminated through measures such as the U.S. Supreme Court decision *Brown v. Board of Education* (1954), which found racially segregated schools to be unconstitutional, and the Civil Rights Acts of the 1960s, which together banned discrimination in public places, schools, employment, voting, and housing. In 1967 the U.S. Supreme

refer to American Nightmare [15]

Court, in *Loving v. Virginia*, ruled that laws prohibiting interracial marriage were unconstitutional, finally eliminating the remaining state laws that made it illegal for whites and blacks to marry each other.

The extent of the problem of racism for African Americans in contemporary society is a topic of heated debate, especially given the election in 2008 of Barack Obama, the first African American president of the United States. *The Economist* magazine claims Obama's election "provided solid evidence that race matters less in America than pessimists suppose."[2] The extent to which race still matters is relevant to determining the extent to which racism is a serious problem in the United States, whether racism is institutionalized in society and culture, whether affirmative action programs should be pursued, and what—if anything—needs to be done about racism. By presenting different views on the extent of racism in the United States and proposed solutions for combating racism, *Current Controversies: Racism* sheds light on this complex and sensitive issue.

Notes

1. C. Loring Brace, "Does Race Exist? An Antagonist's Perspective," *NOVA Online*, November 2000. www.pbs.org. www.pbs.org/wgbh/nova/first/brace.html.

2. *Economist*, "What Will Barack Obama's Presidency Mean for Race Relations?" December 4, 2008. www.economist.com/world/unitedstates/displayStory.cfm?story_id=12725114.

CHAPTER 1

Is Racism a Serious Problem?

Different Views on the Problem of Racism: An Overview

The Economist

The Economist is a British magazine focusing on world business and political analysis and opinion, with a collective staff that writes all articles anonymously.

When Roland Fryer was about 15, a friend asked him what he would be doing when he was 30. He said he would probably be dead. It was a reasonable prediction. At the time, he was hanging out with a gang and selling drugs on the side. Young black men in that line of work seldom live long. But Mr Fryer survived. At 30, he won tenure as an economics professor at Harvard. That was four months ago [in January 2008].

Mr Fryer's parents split up when he was very young. His father was a maths teacher who went off the rails: young Roland once had to borrow money to bail him out of jail. His great-aunt and great-uncle ran a crack business: young Roland would watch them cook cocaine powder into rocks of crack in a frying pan in the kitchen. Several of his relatives went to prison. But Mr Fryer backed away from a life of crime and won a sports scholarship to the University of Texas. He found he enjoyed studying, and was rather good at it. By the time he was 25, the president of Harvard was hectoring him to join the faculty.

The Black-White Gap

Mr Fryer now applies his supple mind to the touchy, tangled issue of racial inequality. Why are African-Americans so much

The Economist, "Nearer to Overcoming," vol. 387, no. 8579, May 10, 2008, p. 38. Copyright © 2008 The Economist Newspaper Ltd. All rights reserved. Republished with permission of The Economist Newspaper Ltd., conveyed through Copyright Clearance Center, Inc.

less prosperous than whites? Why do so many black children flounder in school? Why do so many young black men languish behind bars? Why are stories like Mr Fryer's considered so surprising?

Black life expectancy has soared from 34 in 1900 to 73 today.

Black and white Americans tend to produce different answers to these questions, and there is also heated disagreement within both groups. Some blacks think their glass is three-quarters full; others think it three-quarters empty. Optimists can point to obvious improvements. Little more than four decades ago, blacks in the South could not vote. [In 2008], a black man [was] elected president. Under segregation, southern blacks were barred from white schools, neighbourhoods and opportunities. Now, racial discrimination is both illegal and taboo. Blacks have pierced nearly every glass ceiling. The secretary of state, the boss of American Express and the country's most popular entertainer (Oprah Winfrey) are all black.

Life for the average African-American has also improved remarkably. The median black household income has risen from $22,300 (in 2006 dollars) in 1967 to $32,100 in 2006. Black life expectancy has soared from 34 in 1900 to 73 today. Most blacks today are middle class.

Yes, say the pessimists, but the gap between what blacks and whites earn and what they learn, which narrowed steadily between the 1940s and the late 1980s, has more or less frozen since then. Blacks' median household income is still only 63% of whites'. Academically, black children at 17 perform no better than a white 13-year-old. Blacks die, on average, five years earlier than whites. And though the black middle class has grown immensely, many blacks are still stuck in crime-scorched, nearly jobless ghettos.

Explaining the Gap

What ails black America? Public debate falls between two poles. Some academics and most civil-rights activists stress the role played by racial discrimination. It may no longer be overt, they argue, but it is still widespread and severe. Julian Bond of the National Association for the Advancement of Coloured People reckons that racism is still "epidemic" in America.

Black conservatives, while never denying that racism persists, think it much less severe than before and no longer the main obstacle to black advancement. Bill Cosby, a veteran comedian, tours the country urging blacks to concentrate on improving themselves: to study hard, to work hard and—especially—to shun the culture of despair that grips the ghetto.

The debate is often bitter. Michael Eric Dyson, a leftish academic, argues that the black middle class has "lost its mind" if it believes Mr Cosby's argument downplaying the importance of race. Larry Elder, a conservative pundit, wrote a book about blacks who blame racism for nearly everything called: "Stupid Black Men".

Studiousness is stigmatised among black schoolchildren.

Mr Fryer eschews histrionics in favour of hard data. He is obsessed with education, which he calls "the civil-rights battleground of the 21st century". Why do blacks lag behind whites in school? Mr Fryer is prepared to test even the most taboo proposition. Are blacks genetically predisposed to be less intelligent than whites? With a collaborator from the University of Chicago, Mr Fryer debunked this idea. Granted, blacks score worse than whites on intelligence tests. But Mr Fryer looked at data from new tests on very young children. At eight months to a year, he found almost no racial gap, and that gap disappeared entirely when he added controls for such things as low birth weight.

If the gap is absent in babies, this suggests it is caused by environmental factors, which can presumably be fixed. But first they must be identified. Do black children need better nutrition? More stimulation in the home? Better schools? Probably all these things matter, but how much? "I don't know," says Mr Fryer. It is a phrase that, to his credit, he uses often.

Cool to Be Dumb

His most striking contribution to the debate so far has been to show that black students who study hard are accused of "acting white" and are ostracised by their peers. Teachers have known this for years, at least anecdotally. Mr Fryer found a way to measure it. He looked at a large sample of public-school children who were asked to name their friends. To correct for kids exaggerating their own popularity, he counted a friendship as real only if both parties named each other. He found that for white pupils, the higher their grades, the more popular they were. But blacks with good grades had fewer black friends than their mediocre peers. In other words, studiousness is stigmatised among black schoolchildren. It would be hard to imagine a more crippling cultural norm.

Mr Fryer has some novel ideas about fixing this state of affairs. New York's school system is letting him test a couple of them on its children. One is to give pupils cash incentives. If a nine-year-old completes an exam, he gets $5. For getting the answers right, he gets more money, up to about $250 a year. The notion of bribing children to study makes many parents queasy. Mr Fryer's response is: let's see if it works and drop it if it doesn't.

Another idea, being tested on a different group of children, is to hand out free mobile telephones. The phones do not work during school hours, and children can recharge them with call-minutes only by studying. (The phone companies were happy to help with this.) The phones give the children an incentive to study, and Mr Fryer a means to communicate with them. He talks of "re-branding" academic achievement to make it cool. He knows it will not be easy. He recalls hearing drug-pushers in the 1980s joking "Just say no!" as they handed over the goods, mocking Nancy Reagan's anti-drug slogan.

Racial preferences are unpopular among whites, and the most blatant ones are, increasingly, illegal.

Racial Preferences in Education

Blacks who do well in school are hungrily recruited by universities, which often admit them with lower test scores than are required of whites or Asians. The bar was first lowered for blacks out of a sense that America owes them a debt for past discrimination. Now universities are more likely to argue that racial diversity is valuable for its own sake.

But racial preferences are unpopular among whites, and the most blatant ones are, increasingly, illegal. The University of Michigan used to give applicants more points for being black than for getting a perfect score on the entrance exam. The Supreme Court deemed this unconstitutional in 2003, but ruled that less explicit preferences might be allowable.

When voters are asked if they want to ban racial preferences in the public sphere, they generally say yes. Since the 1990s, three states have passed referendums barring racial preferences, and four more may do so in November [2008— only one state, Nebraska, did so]. Opponents of racial preferences argue that they are bad for blacks, too.

A study by Richard Sander of the University of California, Los Angeles, found that when the bar is lowered for black applicants to law school, they are admitted to institutions where they cannot cope. Many who drop out of top-tier colleges might have thrived at slightly less competitive ones. Mr Sander calculated that the net effect of pro-black preferences was actually to reduce the number of blacks who passed the bar exam. That is, racial preferences for black law students result in fewer black lawyers. John McWhorter, the author of "Winning the Race: Beyond the Crisis in Black America", argues that lowering the bar for blacks also reduces their incentive to excel at school. "As long as black students have to do only so well, they will do only so well," he says.

Blacks and Whites in Employment

For every dollar that a white man earns, a black man makes only 70 cents. Such figures are sometimes bandied around to imply that nearly all of this gap is caused by discrimination. That is bunk. If a firm could really get the same work done 30% more cheaply simply by hiring blacks, someone would have noticed and made a fortune doing just that.

Even when blacks earn as much as whites, the whites are typically far wealthier.

That said, blacks certainly face barriers in the job market. Two economists, Marianne Bertrand and Sendhil Mullainathan, sent out 5,000 replies to job advertisements in Boston and Chicago. Each fictitious applicant was randomly assigned either a black-sounding name, such as Jamal or Lakisha, or a white one, such as Emily or Greg. For every ten jobs the "whites" applied for, they were offered one interview. The "blacks" had to post 15 letters to elicit the same response. Clearly, some managers are racist. But many are not. And many firms are desperate to hire and promote blacks, if only to avoid lawsuits.

Looked at more closely, the statistics are murky. White men are more likely to work than black men. The proportion of black men participating in the labour force fell from 74%

in 1972 to 67% [in 2007]. Whites start more businesses, too. Only 5% of firms are black-owned, though blacks account for 13% of America's population.

A black woman with a degree earns as much as a white woman with a degree. But with a professional degree, the black woman earns 30% more. That does not prove that law firms discriminate in favour of black women—though they may. Another explanation is that a skilled white woman is more likely to have a rich husband (or indeed any husband), and so may have less incentive to maximise her earnings.

Even when blacks earn as much as whites, the whites are typically far wealthier. In 2000 the average white household in the bottom fifth of income-earners had net assets of $24,000. The figure for blacks was a piffling $57. Whites in the middle fifth were five times wealthier than their black counterparts.

Partly this is because whites inherit more. But it is also because of different approaches to investment. Blacks are more likely to put their money in the bank, notes Mr Fryer. Whites are more likely to invest in shares, which generate higher returns. Compound this over a couple of generations and the effect is colossal.

It is not only whites who devalue black lives: black criminals do too.

Other Challenges

Another crucial factor is the collapse of the black family. The proportion of black babies born out of wedlock has nearly doubled since 1970, to 69%. And 70% of these births are to mothers who are truly alone, not cohabiting. Stable two-parent families accumulate wealth more easily than single-parent homes. Two salaries stretch further, two pairs of hands mean less need for paid child care. Two-parent families also find it easier to raise well-adjusted, studious children, who go on to start stable families of their own. Broken families, if middle class, find it harder to stay that way. And if they start in the ghetto, they find it harder to break out.

"Black life is not valued!" booms Michael Walrond, a popular pastor in Harlem. He is referring to the news that three police officers were acquitted of all charges after shooting dead an unarmed black man, Sean Bell, a few hours before his wedding. The cops fired 50 bullets, but the pastor says he is outraged by the figure of 31. Members of his mostly black flock know immediately what he means. Two of the officers were black and all of them thought Mr Bell had a gun. But it was the white officer who reloaded and fired 31 rounds. Mr Walrond's angry sermon draws cheers.

Afterwards, in his office, he agrees that it is not only whites who devalue black lives: black criminals do too. Mr Walrond, like many inner-city clerics, works hard to reform those who stray. But like [President] Barack Obama's former pastor, Jeremiah Wright, he tends to assume the worst about his country. He finds Mr Wright's theory that the government concocted the AIDS virus to kill blacks "credible".

A startling 11% of black males aged 20–34 are behind bars.

He refers to the Tuskegee experiment between 1932 and 1972 when some doctors in Alabama deliberately neglected to treat black syphilis patients in order to study the disease's progression. That was an abomination. But it is hardly evidence that the government is bent on genocide.

From Alienation to Despair

Is the state racist? Those who think so often point to the criminal-justice system. A startling 11% of black males aged 20–34 are behind bars. Overall, black men are seven times more likely to be incarcerated than white men. Until recently, sentences for crack offenders (who are mostly black) were much harsher than those for powder-cocaine offenders (mostly white). Ex-convicts in several states are barred from voting, a penalty that deters no crime but signals to wrongdoers that they can never be full citizens again. "We are becoming a nation of jailers, and racist jailers at that," reckons Glenn Loury, an economist.

Not so, says Heather Mac Donald of the Manhattan Institute, a conservative think-tank. Blacks are more likely to be jailed because they commit more crimes, she argues. In 2005 the black murder rate was seven times higher than that for whites and Latinos combined. Harsh crack laws account only for a smidgeon of the disparity in incarceration rates. In 2006 blacks were 37.5% of state prisoners; exclude drug offenders and that figure drops to 37%. And since black criminals' victims are mostly black, some argue that locking more of them up has saved many black lives.

In other ways, it is far from clear that the government is trying to keep blacks down. Affirmative-action policies mean that it provides jobs for a disproportionate number of them. It also allows blacks who own small businesses to charge 10% more than whites and still win federal contracts. "Small" is generously defined. A firm with 1,500 employees can qualify. Its black owner can be worth $750,000—excluding his home and business—and still be deemed "economically disadvantaged".

Yet many blacks feel alienated in a way that is "vastly disproportionate to real-life stimulus," frets Mr McWhorter. When New Orleans flooded, some speculated that the government had blown up the levees. Even cooler heads believed that the botched response stemmed from [President] George [W.] Bush's indifference to black suffering.

The Effects of Alienation

Alienation has consequences. Amid the revolutionary fervour of the 1960s, says Mr McWhorter, many blacks learned that

"America's racism rendered it unworthy of any self-regarding black person's embrace and that therefore blacks were exempt from mainstream standards of conduct." The conventional wisdom about ghettos—best expressed in William Julius Wilson's book "When Work Disappears"—is that inner cities decayed because factories moved away. But the jobs often moved only a couple of bus rides away. Noting that millions of blacks moved halfway across the country to find work during the "great migration" in the early 20th century, Mr McWhorter wonders why so many of their descendants failed to follow suit.

He offers two explanations. First, a huge expansion of open-ended welfare in the 1960s enabled mothers to subsist without work. Until the mid-1990s, welfare often paid better than an entry-level job. Second, the counter-culture taught young blacks that working for "chump change" was beneath their dignity.

[President] Bill Clinton fixed welfare and pushed millions of jobless women into work. Violent crime has also fallen sharply since the 1990s, despite the best efforts of gangster rappers to glorify it. Previously dysfunctional cities, such as New York and Washington, DC, are now soberly governed and better places to live in.

Yet many African-Americans are intensely gloomy. In a [2007] poll, only 44% said they expected life for blacks to get better, down from 57% in 1986. The subprime mortgage crisis, which will cost many black families their homes [in 2008], will surely deepen the gloom.

Some blacks contend that racism has simply gone underground. Ellis Cose, a journalist, once wrote that even middle-class blacks suffer constant subtle racial slights, and that these are so distressing that they "are in the end most of what life is". Other blacks think he exaggerates. Sometimes, says Mr McWhorter, the assistant trailing you in a store is just trying to sell you something.

The Future of Racism

Taking the longer view, there is much to cheer. In every way that can be measured (a big caveat), racism has diminished in the past two generations. Inter-racial marriages are up seven-fold since 1970. Young Americans are far less likely to express racial animosity than their elders, suggesting that as old bigots die, they will not be replaced. And if Mr Obama becomes president, it would "raise the ceiling for everyone," says Robert Franklin, the president of Morehouse, a black college in Atlanta.

"For me, racism is not going to be an obstacle," says DeWayne Powell, a student at Morehouse. He recalls an incident when, en route to drop off his college application, he stopped to ask for directions. A white receptionist asked sneeringly whether he could read. "I laughed," he says. "I thought: I'm on my way to fulfil my destiny, and you're stuck behind that glass."

The Problem of Racism Is Worse than White America Admits

Andrew Stephen

Andrew Stephen is U.S. editor of the New Statesman *and a regular contributor to BBC news programs and* The Sunday Times Magazine.

You have to drive 223 miles north-west of New Orleans and deep into the heart of Louisiana before you finally reach the town, which has a population of just 3,000. "Welcome to Jena," says the signpost. "A Nice Place To Call Home." True, it has a McDonald's and a Wal-Mart if you like that sort of thing; but it is also poor and determinedly white, with an annual per-capita income of less than $14,000, and just 12 per cent of its population is black. That means white people still rule Jena: civil rights reforms have passed it by, and housing, churches and even the cemetery are rigidly segregated. It is part of LaSalle Parish, which back in 1991 cast 4,910 votes for David Duke—a former Ku Klux Klan grand wizard and admirer of Hitler—and only 2,432 for the previous and future Democratic governor of Louisiana.

Thanks to word of mouth, the unstinting attention of black radio stations and (at last) muted coverage from the mainstream media, however, Jena is fast becoming as disconcertingly symbolic of 21st-century racial turmoil as places like Little Rock, Selma and Montgomery were in the 20th century. On a slow-moving march [in September 2007] that stretched for miles beyond Jena itself, leaders such as the Reverends Jesse Jackson, Al Sharpton and Martin Luther King III linked arms with countless thousands of demonstrators to protest

Andrew Stephen, "The Deep South, the White Tree, the Noose," *New Statesman*, vol. 136, October 29, 2007, pp. 26–28. Copyright © 2007 New Statesman, Ltd. Reproduced by permission.

against what they see as the racism, hatred and injustice evoked by Jena. The likes of the rappers Mos Def, Salt 'n' Pepa and Ice Cube joined them; and the rock singer John Cougar Mellencamp has already become the Joan Baez of this new era, singing his protest song "Jena" when he performed at the opening game in the NFL season on 6 September [2007].

The Reality of Racism

I will come to the reasons why Jena symbolises what Jackson calls "a defining moment" in the 21st-century civil rights movement shortly. First, however, a brief personal experience. [In 2006] I wrote a long article for the *Washington Post* about slavery and its legacy of present-day racism, and found myself overwhelmed with emails from readers; two more, in fact, arrived just last week [in October 2007]. Besides those from the usual crackpots and from middle-class white folk expressing polite scepticism, the overwhelming majority were from black people, repeating over and over again the same message, something like: "We already knew all about this, but thanks for bringing it to a wider audience."

A foreigner, it seemed, had exposed an issue rarely faced here, in the newspaper of the nation's capital or elsewhere in the white media. I found myself appearing on coast-to-coast black radio shows I didn't even know existed—hosted by black broadcasters such as Michael Baisden and Tom Joyner, whom I later discovered were prominent early voices exposing the Jena scandals—and I realised, after almost two decades of living in the United States and complacently assuming that race relations were steadily improving, that so much of the 13 per cent of America that is black still considers itself ignored, forgotten and unheard in the white world that surrounds it.

"The real question here is why is there such a hunger in America to be lied to about race?" is how Tom Wolfe posed the conundrum two decades ago. Like anti-Semitism, racism in America today is rife but has been driven underground since the 1964–65 legal reforms that followed the cataclysms of Birmingham, Selma and Montgomery. The statistics speak for themselves: black people are still perceived today as *threats*, human dangers that have to be kept down and contained, as they were from the earliest days of slavery.

No less an authority than the US justice department tells us that a black man in 2007 is three times more likely to be sent to prison than a white man; half the country's prison population is black, and one in three black men in their thirties has a prison record. A black person is three times more likely to have his or her car searched than a white one, and black people are meted out prison sentences 20 per cent longer on average than those their white peers receive for identical crimes. Whites use illegal drugs more than blacks, but blacks are still 2.5 times more likely to be arrested for drugs offences.

The noose is symbol of 4,743 documented lynchings between 1882 and 1968.

The Noose in Jena

I can already hear the sublimated voices of the James Watsons of this world, whispering that this is all because black people have genetically lower IQs and are more disposed to crime. I invite Professor Watson to leave his Long Island lab and come down to Jena to investigate racial realities for himself—reading, for example, the handwritten witness statements of both black and white teenagers concerned in the so-called "Jena Six" tragedy. Having done so myself, I can say that those of the white youths involved are noticeably even more illiterate.

The saga began on 31 August [2006], when a new black teenage pupil at Jena High School named Kenneth Purvis asked an assistant principal if he was allowed to sit under a large oak in the school grounds known as "the white tree"— where only white kids, usually, shaded themselves from the searing hot sun of the Deep South. He was told he could, and duly did so. Next morning two (possibly three) nooses were found hanging from the tree's branches, draped in school colours. The noose is symbol of 4,743 documented lynchings between 1882 and 1968—hundreds of them, at the very least, in Louisiana.

Three white boys were soon identified as the culprits and the principal tried to expel them, but his decision was overturned by the school's "expulsion committee". Black students staged an impromptu protest under the tree and when police moved in with LaSalle's district attorney, one Reed Waters, a school assembly was called. "See this pen?" Waters asked the kids rhetorically. "I can end your lives with a pen." Waters later denied that he was specifically addressing the black youngsters, but white and black students alike—their outlooks conditioned by generations of racist hatred and violence—had few doubts about whom he was addressing.

Theft of a Firearm

Tensions simmered until the end of the football season—one of the few diversions available for Jena teenagers—but on 1 December, five black schoolboys tried to join a Friday-night party in the town attended by both whites and blacks. Seventeen-year-old Robert Bailey, one of the black youths, was immediately attacked outside (with a beer bottle, he said later) by a 22-year-old white man, who was subsequently put on probation for assault.

The next day Bailey and two other black kids from Jena High were in the Gotta-Go Grocery store when a white schoolmate who had been at the party the previous night approached them; the white boy, Matt Windham, says he was threatened by the three others, but acknowledges that he then went outside to his truck to fetch a 12-gauge riot shotgun that had been specially equipped with a black laser sight. Bailey and his two friends wrestled the gun away from Windham but were subsequently charged with theft of a firearm, second-degree robbery and disturbing the peace. Windham was never arrested or charged with anything whatsoever.

Back at Jena High the following Monday lunchtime, a 17-year-old white boy called Justin Barker started taunting Bailey in the school gym for having had his "ass whipped" by a white man the previous Friday night. Moments later, says Barker in his handwritten police statement (and you think I'm exaggerating when I write about the declining standards of US education?), "Me and my girl frend was walking out of the gym and a group of blacks was standing out side the door and when we got out of the door i told my girl frend to tern left to go up the side walk and when I ternt my back to the one of them sad this will teech you to run your Fucken mouth and that was it."

The Attack

It was certainly a vicious attack: Robert Bailey, his two friends who had been with him at the Gotta-Go Grocery and three or four other black teenage boys now stand accused of ambushing Barker outside the gym and of punching and kicking him unconscious. Barker's girlfriend, in her own handwriting, takes up the story: "When he got nnocked out they still kicked him just as heard! When I saw what was goen on I started yelling ... I grabed on of there arms and pulled him away! Well, I tryed!" Barker was treated at the local hospital for three hours for concussion, an eye that had swollen shut, and cuts and bruises to his face, ears and hand; but what is indisputable is that he felt well enough to attend Jena High's ring ceremony for departing seniors that evening.

Enter, at this point, the sternly unyielding white-authority figure of DA Reed Waters. He promptly charged Bailey and five others with *attempted murder* as well as conspiracy to commit murder, charges that carry mandatory sentences of ten to 50 years' hard labour with no chance of probation or parole. The black men, ranging in this case from 14 to 18 years of age, represented those ever-present threats that had to be kept down and contained, you see. Waters insisted on charging Mychal Bell, 16, as an adult because he had a police record and had initiated the attack, Waters claimed.

Nooses . . . are now proliferating at the homes and workplaces of black people here, there and everywhere.

The charges were subsequently reduced to aggravated battery and conspiracy. But Bell's trial [in June 2007], the first of the six that was presided over by an all-white jury (none of the potential black jurors turned up, according to the authorities), still presented Waters with a problem. Legally, a "deadly weapon" had to be used in aggravated battery. Waters therefore argued that the humdrum tennis shoes Bell was wearing at the time of the assault on Barker constituted deadly weapons, an argument the jury found persuasive. Bell was duly pronounced guilty, but appeal courts subsequently ruled that he should never have been tried as an adult in the first place. . . . Trials for the remaining five have yet to be scheduled [Bell was sentenced to 18 months in a juvenile facility on October 11, 2007].

The Aftermath of Jena

Nooses, those most terrifying symbols of white American aggression during the Jim Crow century that was supposed to have ended in the aftermath of the Birmingham and Selma mutinies, are now proliferating at the homes and workplaces of black people here, there and everywhere. The FBI has set up a special task force to try to stamp down on what is fast threatening to become the 21st-century version of burning crosses or Nazi swastikas. Now that the mainstream media are belatedly paying attention to what has been happening in Jena, so politicians, too, are sitting up. The federal House judiciary committee held its first hearing on the events [in January 2008. Waters and most Republicans declined to attend.

None of these [post–Civil War] amendments or [civil rights] acts worked as well as they should have done in ridding America of the poisonous racism that still runs through its bloodstream.

Bell is still only 17 but has no hope of pursuing the career as a professional footballer that was a very real possibility not so long ago. He was released from prison on 27 September on $45,000 bail after being held for ten months on the Barker charges. Within a fortnight, however, he was back in a cell after yet another Louisiana judge ruled that he had violated his probation on unrelated charges. Meanwhile, two of the other defendants were greeted with a standing ovation when they appeared on stage at the Black Entertainment Television (BET) Hip-Hop Awards in Atlanta on 13 October [2007]: a potent visual symbol of America's racial divisions that would have horrified most white Americans, had they been watching BET.

The outcome of America's civil war (1861–65) was the passage of the 13th, 14th and 15th amendments between 1865 and 1870, outlawing slavery, granting full citizenship to everybody born in the US and giving the vote to all (men). The revolts of Birmingham in 1963 and Selma in 1965 led to the Civil Rights Act and Voting Rights Act, respectively. None of these amendments or acts worked as well as they should have done in ridding America of the poisonous racism that still runs through its bloodstream. But might the 21st-century uprisings in Jena, I wonder, at last lead to truly significant progress?

Today's Racial Inequalities Are a Product of America's Racist Past

Maryann Cusimano Love

Maryann Cusimano Love is associate professor of international politics at Catholic University in Washington, D.C.

As Senator Barack Obama explores a presidential bid [in 2007 and 2008], media headlines across the country ask, "Is America ready for an African-American president?" Between 50 percent and 62 percent of Americans polled answer yes, that race is no longer a barrier in the United States. But that this is considered a newsworthy headline by all the major media outlets and that around 40 percent of those polled answer no suggests otherwise. A recent controversy in Virginia echoes the issue. A Virginia state legislator, Delegate Frank D. Hargrove Sr., a Republican from a suburb of Richmond, gave a newspaper interview on Martin Luther King Jr. Day in which he said that "blacks need to get over" slavery. He was stating his opposition to a resolution in the Virginia legislature to apologize for slavery and promote racial reconciliation as part of Virginia's activities marking the 400th anniversary of the English settlement at Jamestown in 1607. Officials tout Jamestown's founding as the birthplace of our nation (predating the pilgrims' landing in Plymouth Rock by 13 years), of representative government, of the rule of law and of American entrepreneurism. (Jamestown was settled by the Virginia Company of London in order to bring profits back to shareholders.) But Jamestown was also the birthplace of slavery in our country. Government time and tax money are be-

Maryann Cusimano Love, "Race in America: 'We Would Like to Believe We Are Over the Problem,'" *America*, vol. 196, no. 5, February 12, 2007, p. 8. Copyright © 2007 www.americamagazine.org. All rights reserved. Reproduced by permission of America Press. For subscription information, call 212-581-4640 or visit www.americamagazine .org.

ing spent on the commemoration. One sponsor of the resolution, state Senator Henry Marsh, notes that while "the whole world's attention is on Virginia" because of the Jamestown anniversary, "Virginia can take a leadership role in promoting racial harmony." Delegate Hargrove disagrees. He argues it is "counterproductive to dwell on it," noting that "not a soul today had anything to do with slavery."

The Relevance of the Past

Some of Delegate Hargrove's argument is attractive. It lets us all off the hook for the inequities of the past. My Sicilian and Irish great-grandparents emigrated to the United States in the 1900's. By Hargrove's logic, my family is not responsible for slavery or its aftermath, because we were not here when it happened. On the other hand, my husband's family moved from Scotland and Ireland to the Chesapeake Bay region in the 1600's. We know little of the family history, but the name is common in these parts, on both black and white faces. I laugh in the grocery checkout lane with an African-American over our shared name, Love. But later, I wonder—are we related? Did someone in my family tree own someone in your family tree?

To "get over" racial problems in America today, we need to understand them and their roots.

The flaw in Hargrove's argument is that the inequities of the past persist today. Noting the achievements of African-Americans like Senator Obama, we would like to believe that we "are over" the race problem. But the statistics paint a more sobering picture. Dr. David Satcher, the 16th surgeon general of the United States, notes that 85,000 African-Americans died in the year 2000 due to inequality in health care. The infant mortality rate of black babies is double the infant mortality rate of white babies in the United States. African-Americans have lower life expectancies than white Americans by six or seven years. Twenty-five percent of black Americans live in poverty. One-third of African-American children live in poverty. Black poverty rates are triple those of whites. Tavis Smiley's book, *Covenant with Black America,* explores many other disturbing inequities that persist in the United States today in housing, education and the criminal justice system. The *Hatewatch* Web site lists cross burnings and activities of white supremacist groups today, and it is possible to track the hate groups currently active in each state. The Harvard online racial bias tests have shown that millions of Americans harbor racial preconceptions. And 16-year-old Kiri Davis repeated the "doll test" used in the 1954 *Brown v. Board of Education* case with the same infamous results: 4- and 5-year-old black children in Harlem overwhelmingly said that the black dolls were bad and the white dolls were good and pretty. As past inequities continue into the present, we have a moral responsibility to address them.

Understanding Is Needed

To "get over" racial problems in America today, we need to understand them and their roots. But we don't. A recent survey conducted by the University of Connecticut found that more than 19 percent of the 14,000 college students in 50 U.S. universities surveyed believed that Martin Luther King Jr.'s "I Have a Dream" speech was advocating the abolition of slavery. I teach a course at Catholic University on the civil rights movement. Our students, most of them graduates of Catholic elementary and high schools, know little of U.S. or Catholic racial history.

The United States is not alone. Such debates are hallmarks of peacebuilding efforts in post-conflict societies from South Africa to Colombia. We all face these choices, balancing apologies, reconciliation, redress for past wrongs, with attention to present and future problems.

Delegate Hargrove's suggestion that we "get over" the past by not bringing it up can be tempting because it is easy. Senator Obama's vision of a post-racial politics is inviting because it is hopeful. But we are not there yet, and the only way to get there is to work through the present-day ramifications of our persistent past, not only as individuals ("*I* don't condone racism") but as communities ("What are *we* doing to end unacceptable racial inequities?").

Racism Remains a Reality in American Culture

National Catholic Reporter

National Catholic Reporter is an independent weekly newspaper reporting on issues important to Catholics.

Don Imus, aptly designated a "shock jock," contributes significantly to the aural litter that increasingly jams our airways. There is little in his background that might recommend him to the masses as a thinker, an analyst or even an engaging conversational partner. His low-grade mumbling provides a kind of counterpoint to the abundant screaming heads who attempt to insinuate themselves into arenas of serious discourse. That and a gift for junior high-level locker-room banter are major distinguishing characteristics.

Shock Jocks and Politicians

He sits apart because he is inexplicably popular, drawing millions of listeners daily, and because, just as inexplicably, he has been coddled by some of the country's highest profile journalists and politicians. Were Imus a politician himself, many of those who count themselves among the mainstream world of white male journalism, and who are shameless in participating in his morning show and its strange brand of humor, would long ago have called for his head.

Consult Mississippi [senator] Trent Lott for what occurs when a politician allows the ignorant bigotry of a largely bygone age to sprout anew. At a 100th birthday party in 2002 for the now late Sen. Strom Thurmond, Lott remarked: "When Strom Thurmond ran for president, we voted for him. We're proud of it. And if the rest of the country had followed our lead, we wouldn't have had all these problems over all these years, either."

Lott got into trouble not for some direct racial slur, but because his remarks indicated that he supported the ideas behind Thurmond's failed candidacy during which the noted bigot had declared: "All the laws of Washington and all the bayonets of the Army cannot force the negro into our homes, our schools, our churches." His party platform announced: "We stand for the segregation of the races and the racial integrity of each race."

Lott, who came under enormous pressure for his comments, eventually was forced down as Senate majority leader.

The Reaction to Imus

In time it may become apparent why, after decades of spewing hateful racist, homophobic and sexist prattle, Imus finally got caught up short when he referred to the Rutgers University women's basketball team as "nappy-headed hos."

What is important, however, is not "Why now?" but what it means that any major broadcast figure would traffick in such trash and that some elements of the culture would finally react with enough force to jeopardize his career.

In 1999, *NCR* [*National Catholic Reporter*] ran a story quoting longtime Imus critic Philip Nobile, who said no one could escape "the racist, sexist and homophobic rhetoric" that was stock-in-trade for the shock jock and his crew.

Nobile at the time was campaigning to convince a priest and a rabbi, who referred to themselves as the "God Squad," to stop appearing on Imus' show, where they discussed religion.

In a letter to the local bishop at the time, Nobile said the Imus show "routinely smears racial minorities, homosexuals and the handicapped with vicious and vile remarks that should shock Catholic conscience."

In a precursor to some of the defense offered by media biggies today, the priest, [Monsignor] Tom Hartman, told *NCR* at the time that Imus did a lot for disadvantaged kids and that "he's doing a real good job with his soul" despite his "locker room, bad boy style."

We're not out to judge anyone's soul, just the content of the material that's broadcast.

In the case of the remarks about the Rutgers women, it is enough to say that the remarks were vile and demeaning to all women and people of color.

The Positive Results

Whatever happens during upcoming meetings and what the Web site *TomPaine.com* characterized as the "Don Imus groveling and penitence tour," several beneficial developments could result.

The culture has been forced once again to confront the fact that racism . . . remains a disturbing reality in America.

The first is that the incident has spotlighted the accomplishments and the humanity of the group of successful student athletes from Rutgers. This is a case where insults are rendered all the more absurd because of the young women's accomplishments and their prospects for the future.

Second, the long history of Imus' bigotry and lack of discretion has been bared. The lesson is that free speech misused can have a downside, and in this case a good example of how that downside works is being demonstrated. At presstime the marketplace was already beginning to distance itself from the Imus world. Corporations were pulling their ads. While principled discussion often fails, economic loss can make the point with the Imuses of the world.

Finally, but certainly not of least consequence, the culture has been forced once again to confront the fact that racism, while not as prevalent or public as during the era of Thurmond's presidential bid, remains a disturbing reality in America. That division is a fundamental sin of the culture, a fault line that can lie dangerously hidden, its spasms unpredictable. No matter how unsettling the jolts that bring the reality of racism to the surface, the more we are forced to confront it and talk about it, the better the chance that eventually the breach can be healed.

The Role of Racism in America Is Overstated

John McWhorter

John McWhorter writes and comments extensively on race and ethnicity as a senior fellow for the Manhattan Institute and is the author of Winning the Race: Beyond the Crisis in Black America.

"We have an amazing tolerance for black pain," Jesse Jackson told CNN, implying that the Hurricane Katrina relief effort was delayed because those who were hardest hit were poor and black. Jackson elsewhere drove the point home by comparing the New Orleans convention center, where the refugees were first gathered, to "the hull of a slave ship." Shortly thereafter rapper Kanye West went off-script on an NBC special intended to raise money for the rescue effort. He informed us that "It's been five days because most of the people are black. George [W.] Bush doesn't care about black people."

The Charge of Racism

Others have conveyed the point by implication. [Representative] Elijah Cummings, when asked on CNN whether racism played a role, said, "I'm not sure. All I know is that a number of the faces that I saw were African-American." Meanwhile, Rep. Diane Watson took issue with calling survivors "refugees": "'Refugee' calls up to mind people that come from different lands and have to be taken care of. These are American citizens." For anyone who thinks that the rescuers saw blacks as less than fellow citizens, the meaning behind Watson's lexicography lesson came through loud and clear.

John McWhorter, "'Racism!' They Charged," *National Review*, vol. 57, no. 17, September 26, 2005, pp. 26, 28. Copyright © 2005 by National Review, Inc., 215 Lexington Avenue, New York, NY 10016. Reproduced by permission.

No one will deny that what we have seen on our television screens points to the tragic realities of racial disparity, in an unusually stark way. The almost all-black crowds sweltering, starving, and dying in the convention center have shown us that in New Orleans, as in so many other places, to be poor is often to be black. There is a debate to be had on whether this reality is the legacy of racism—either past or present—but as we face the prospect of finding many thousands of dead as the waters recede, historical debates of this kind can and should wait.

To claim that racism is the reason that the rescue effort was so slow is not a matter of debate at all: It's nothing more than a handy way to get media attention, or to help sell a new CD. It's self-affirming, too, if playing the victim is the only way you know to make yourself feel like you matter.

It is also absurd.

American Disasters

To say "George Bush doesn't care about black people" means that one honestly believes that if it were the poor whites of Louisiana who happened to live closest to the levees, hardly anyone would have gotten wet. Fifty thousand troops would have been standing at the borders of the city as soon as Katrina popped up on meteorologists' radar screens. The National Guard would have magically lifted the long-entrenched bureaucratic restrictions that allow states to call up troops only when it is proven that they are needed. The U.S. Navy would have anticipated that refugees would number in the tens of thousands, and would have started the days-long process of loading up rescue ships with supplies a week before the storm actually hit. Suddenly, against all historical precedent, just for that week, the Federal Emergency Management Agency [FEMA] would have morphed into a well-organized and dependable outfit.

What previous example is this scenario based on? Surely people who level so trenchant a claim have some precedent in mind. For example, what about the hurricane that Katrina has just displaced as the third strongest on record to hit America? Ground zero for Hurricane Andrew, which left 250,000 people homeless, was Homestead, [Florida,] where whites were a strong majority. So was help pouring in as soon as the rain stopped?

There will be those who will insist, no matter what the evidence, that racism slowed the rescue effort.

Not exactly. Few people remember Kate Hale, who had her 15 minutes of fame as the Dade County emergency-management director who asked on national television, "Where in the hell is the cavalry on this one?" People went without electricity or food and dealt with looters for, as it happens, five days—just as in New Orleans. FEMA was raked over the coals for the same bureaucratic incompetence that is making headlines now.

Is it so farfetched to admit that the problem here was the general ineptness of America's defenses against unforeseen disasters? One is inclined to consider the attacks of 9/11. Two presidential administrations neglected increasingly clear signs that Osama bin Laden was planning to attack us on our shores. It's unlikely that anyone supposes that had anything to do with racial bigotry (Clinton was our "first black president," after all). In general, bureaucracies are notoriously bad at foresight and long-term planning, and FEMA has never exactly offered a counter-example.

What Could Be

Of course, there will be those who will insist, no matter what the evidence, that racism slowed the rescue effort. They should, however, do more than strike poses: They should channel their alienation into something more constructive. As hundreds of thousands of poor blacks return to their home city, where so much will have to be rebuilt from square one, this could be an opportunity to create a coherent all-black enclave that warms the hearts of "black nationalists." With the massive funding from Washington that the reconstruction will require, New Orleans can build new schools with fresh supplies and modern equipment. Welfare-to-work programs can be beefed up with better provisions for childcare. For years to come, the city will offer ample opportunities for poor blacks to get training in construction, white-collar jobs, and—tragically, but usefully—medical and foster care. There will also be an unprecedented chance to create small businesses to serve the community as it rebuilds.

The result could be a thriving black working class in New Orleans. Older blacks fondly recall the struggling but coherent black communities that integration dissolved—sometimes a little "segregation" can be a good thing.

New Orleans is where Homer Plessy boarded a first-class train coach in 1892, which sparked the *Plessy v. Ferguson* Supreme Court decision that legalized segregation nationwide. The Ninth Ward that Katrina pounded was the same Ninth Ward where four black first-grade girls braved racist taunts on national television in 1960, as they took their places in all-white schools. Couldn't the Congressional Black Caucus take this as an opportunity for activism both symbolic and proactive, and work with Louisiana and New Orleans to channel billions of dollars into making a real-life Chocolate City?

People inclined to see "racism" peeking out from behind every rock and tree tend to think poor blacks will be saved only by a Second Civil Rights Revolution. They might take the aftermath of Katrina as the closest thing the real world will ever give them to realizing that dream: a chance to create a strong, working-class black community from the ground up.

Alternatively, one could sit back and savor this moment as an opportunity for the idle catharsis that goes along with the calisthenics of identity politics. That would substitute for the real work of improving people's lives, the cheap thrills of feeling good—the Big Easy, indeed.

Racial Inequalities Are the Product of Culture, Not Racism

Thomas Sowell

Thomas Sowell is the Rose and Milton Friedman Senior Fellow at the Hoover Institution and the author of Black Rednecks and White Liberals.

For most of the history of this country, differences between the black and the white population—whether in income, IQ, crime rates, or whatever—have been attributed to either race or racism. For much of the first half of the 20th century, these differences were attributed to race—that is, to an assumption that blacks just did not have it in their genes to do as well as white people. The tide began to turn in the second half of the 20th century, when the assumption developed that black-white differences were due to racism on the part of whites.

Three decades of my own research lead me to believe that neither of those explanations will stand up under scrutiny of the facts. As one small example, a study published [in 2004] indicated that most of the black alumni of Harvard were from either the West Indies or Africa, or were the children of West Indian or African immigrants. These people are the same race as American blacks, who greatly outnumber either or both.

If this disparity is not due to race, it is equally hard to explain by racism. To a racist, one black is pretty much the same as another. But, even if a racist somehow let his racism stop at the water's edge, how could he tell which student was the son or daughter of someone born in the West Indies or in Africa,

Thomas Sowell, "Crippled by Their Culture," *Wall Street Journal*, April 26, 2005, p. A14.

especially since their American-born offspring probably do not even have a foreign accent?

What then could explain such large disparities in demographic "representation" among these three groups of blacks? Perhaps they have different patterns of behavior and different cultures and values behind their behavior.

The Culture of the South

There have always been large disparities, even within the native black population of the U.S. Those blacks whose ancestors were "free persons of color" in 1850 have fared far better in income, occupation, and family stability than those blacks whose ancestors were freed in the next decade by Abraham Lincoln.

What is not nearly as widely known is that there were also very large disparities within the white population of the pre–Civil War South and the white population of the Northern states. Although Southern whites were only about one-third of the white population of the U.S., an absolute majority of all the illiterate whites in the country were in the South.

Slavery doesn't stand up under scrutiny of historical facts any better than race or racism as explanations of North-South differences or black-white differences.

The North had four times as many schools as the South, attended by more than four times as many students. Children in Massachusetts spent more than twice as many years in school as children in Virginia. Such disparities obviously produce other disparities. Northern newspapers had more than four times the circulation of Southern newspapers. Only 8% of the patents issued in 1851 went to Southerners. Even though agriculture was the principal economic activity of the antebellum South at the time, the vast majority of the patents for agricultural inventions went to Northerners. Even the cotton gin was invented by a Northerner.

Disparities between Southern whites and Northern whites extended across the board from rates of violence to rates of illegitimacy. American writers from both the antebellum South and the North commented on the great differences between the white people in the two regions. So did famed French visitor Alexis de Tocqueville.

None of these disparities can be attributed to either race or racism. Many contemporary observers attributed these differences to the existence of slavery in the South, as many in later times would likewise attribute both the difference between Northern and Southern whites, and between blacks and whites nationwide, to slavery. But slavery doesn't stand up under scrutiny of historical facts any better than race or racism as explanations of North-South differences or black-white differences. The people who settled in the South came from different regions of Britain than the people who settled in the North—and they differed as radically on the other side of the Atlantic as they did here—that is, before they had ever seen a black slave.

Culture, Not Slavery

Slavery also cannot explain the difference between American blacks and West Indian blacks living in the United States because the ancestors of both were enslaved. When race, racism, and slavery all fail the empirical test, what is left?

Culture is left.

The culture of the people who were called "rednecks" and "crackers" before they ever got on the boats to cross the Atlantic was a culture that produced far lower levels of intellectual and economic achievement, as well as far higher levels of violence and sexual promiscuity. That culture had its own way of talking, not only in the pronunciation of particular words but also in a loud, dramatic style of oratory with vivid imagery, repetitive phrases and repetitive cadences.

Although that style originated on the other side of the Atlantic in centuries past, it became for generations the style of both religious oratory and political oratory among Southern whites and among Southern blacks—not only in the South but in the Northern ghettos in which Southern blacks settled. It was a style used by Southern white politicians in the era of Jim Crow and later by black civil rights leaders fighting Jim Crow. Martin Luther King's famous speech at the Lincoln Memorial in 1963 was a classic example of that style.

While a third of the white population of the U.S. lived within the redneck culture, more than 90% of the black population did. Although that culture eroded away over the generations, it did so at different rates in different places and among different people. It eroded away much faster in Britain than in the U.S. and somewhat faster among Southern whites than among Southern blacks, who had fewer opportunities for education or for the rewards that came with escape from that counterproductive culture.

The redneck culture proved to be a major handicap for both whites and blacks who absorbed it.

Nevertheless the process took a long time. As late as the First World War, white soldiers from Georgia, Arkansas, Kentucky and Mississippi scored lower on mental tests than black soldiers from Ohio, Illinois, New York and Pennsylvania. Again, neither race nor racism can explain that—and neither can slavery.

The redneck culture proved to be a major handicap for both whites and blacks who absorbed it. Today, the last remnants of that culture can still be found in the worst of the black ghettos, whether in the North or the South, for the ghettos of the North were settled by blacks from the South.

The counterproductive and self-destructive culture of black rednecks in today's ghettos is regarded by many as the only "authentic" black culture—and, for that reason, something not to be tampered with. Their talk, their attitudes, and their behavior are regarded as sacrosanct.

The people who take this view may think of themselves as friends of blacks. But they are the kinds of friends who can do more harm than enemies.

Racism in America Is Waning

Dan Rodricks

Dan Rodricks is a columnist for The Baltimore Sun *newspaper.*

I think it's fair to say that every white American knows another white American who is a bigot. The bigotry comes out in different ways—in conversation about politics, sports, crime, music, life in general. The bigot you know probably enjoys sharing a crude joke now and then, and these days you might receive an offensive e-mail from him, as I did [recently].

If you've been around this person enough over the years, you pretty much know what to expect. You don't expect this person to change. You don't expect this person to say anything nice about, much less vote for, Barack Obama. (He or she probably didn't have many pleasant words about Hillary Clinton, either.)

I would also say this: Every white American of a certain age—say 40 to 60—knows fewer bigots today than he or she did 20 years ago because, for one thing, a lot of them have died off. We have become a more tolerant society by generational attrition. But there's more to it than that. We're far from colorblind, but if Obama's presidential nomination signals anything, it's at least the dawn of a new era in this changing nation.

The Younger Generations

Baby boomers grew up immersed in racial bigotry—most of us were born when Jim Crow laws were still on the books—but our kids are growing up in what the pollster John Zogby calls a "beige America."

Our kids have not had the instruction in racial hatred a lot of their parents and grandparents had. More than ever before, Gen[eration] X and Gen Y are the offspring of mixed-race and ethnically mixed couples.

More of them have been exposed to greater ethnic and racial diversity in their schools, in their musical choices and cultural interests, at work, and through the global reach of the Internet. They've made Will Smith the top-rated, highest-paid movie star and Tiger Woods one of the most popular sports figures of their time.

In his first book, *The Way We'll Be*, Zogby predicts that Americans who are now between 18 and 29 will be the first colorblind generation. He calls them the "first globals," young Americans who are acquiring an "expansive world view" as they mature. They are better educated and more connected to the world than previous generations. They have a greater appreciation of the need for international cooperation, mainly because of environmental and human rights issues.

There has been profound cultural change in the 40 years since the civil rights movement and the statutory end of "separate but equal."

The "first globals" are consumers, to be sure, but they are less likely to define the American dream in terms of materialism. They don't expect to live as well as their parents or grandparents did, but they consider personal fulfillment a top priority. Zogby believes the "first globals" are leading America to "a new age of inclusion and authenticity."

This sounds like wishful thinking, but it's based on Zogby Interactive's comprehensive polling system. Others have noticed this transformation.

So it isn't just time and death that is reducing the number of bigots and making America a more accepting society. There has been profound cultural change in the 40 years since the civil rights movement and the statutory end of "separate but equal." We're making progress. Obama is the latest sign of it.

But are we there yet?

A Measure of Progress

"What else explains why this is even a close race?" a friend, who is black, said over lunch the other day. "After eight years of [President George W.] Bush, with the war, with the gas prices, with the economy going the way it is, what else would explain why John McCain is even close to Barack Obama in the polls?"

I had just described for him an e-mail I received—forwarded several times and ultimately from someone I know—that is one of the most blatantly racist I've seen this year, playing on bigoted stereotypes about the African-American work ethic. White bigots would find it funny. Everyone else would be offended by it. After seeing this garbage—and others that have come through the Internet—you can appreciate why a middle-age black man sitting in a restaurant in Baltimore would view the 2008 presidential election as a measure of the degree of racism in America.

But it's also a measure of our racial progress, though, for most of this extraordinary campaign year [2008], that has not been the way Obama's candidacy was framed. Before the [Reverend] Jeremiah Wright episode, when Obama was forced to take on race with that phenomenal speech in Philadelphia, the primary-season debates had been all about the issues with which Americans should be most concerned—the cost of health care, energy policy, the war in Iraq—and not race. The war, the economy and health care are the things that should be on the minds of all Americans, no matter what their race or party affiliation, as the clock ticks toward November. Everything else is a sideshow.

"I think there's a silent longing for an American catharsis on race," my friend added. "Racial bigotry has been a long and strong and sad part of our nation's history. Many Americans want our country to grow up."

As for the bigots, my friend and I agreed: There isn't much you can do about them. The older ones, in particular, are not going to change. If the bigot you know forwards you a racist e-mail, you should respond by telling him or her that it's sick and stupid and should stop. Then hit the delete key. Do not forward these e-mails, even to friends as evidence of the evil lurking in our midst. Forwarding them just spreads the poison, and that's the last thing a country facing huge problems needs right now.

CHAPTER 2

Is Racism Institutionalized in Society and Culture?

Chapter Preface

When people think of racism, often one of the first images that comes to mind is a specific racist act between individuals; for example, one person might verbally attack another with a racial slur, sending a negative message about the targeted person based on his or her race. Whereas this kind of racism occurs among individuals and is blatant, institutional racism occurs at the level of social institutions and can be more subtle and insidious. Institutional racism is defined as racism that is structured into political and social institutions; for example, a health care system may be structured in a way that denies racial minorities adequate treatment by excluding from a managed care network sections of a city where racial minorities happen to live. In such a case, while individuals within the system might not be racist, the structure of the system itself results in racial discrimination. One area where the charge of institutional racism has been leveled is that of standardized testing.

Standardized testing takes place both in primary and secondary education (K–12), as well as for admission into post-secondary schooling such as college and graduate school. California, for instance, has a Standardized Testing and Reporting Program (STAR) that administers the California Standards Tests (CSTs) for grades two through eleven. Examples of standardized testing for entrance into post-secondary schooling include the SAT Reasoning Test (for college admission); the Graduate Record Examination, or GRE (for graduate school admission); the Medical College Admission Test, or MCAT; and the Law School Admission Test, or LSAT. Given the importance of these tests for students and applicants, it is important that the tests not display bias against any group of individuals. Debate about this issue has arisen with respect to many standardized tests; in recent years a controversy erupted over the LSAT.

The evidence that prompted differing hypotheses about the potential bias in the LSAT concerned data showing that minority students from prestigious universities scored well below white counterparts who had received similar grades in similar majors from the same universities. One explanation is that the LSAT is racially biased, containing questions that favor the experience of whites over that of racial minorities, a hypothesis endorsed by David M. White, founder of the non-profit corporation Testing for the Public. Social commentator Stanley Kurtz, however, argues that this theory is nonsense, suggesting that professors at the elite colleges in question may have inflated the grades given to minority students admitted under affirmative action, thereby explaining the gap: "It is at just such schools where affirmative action is practiced most assiduously, and where minority students are most likely to be admitted without adequate preparation—and with vastly lower SAT scores."

Determining whether the LSAT contains racial bias demands close attention to not only the dissimilar test results, but also to the test itself. As Kurtz's alternative hypothesis shows, the difference in test scores alone may not show that bias exists. To determine whether or not the LSAT actually is racially biased, these two hypotheses and others would need to be more deeply explored. Debates about the existence of institutional racism require careful consideration of the evidence and possible causes. The viewpoints in this chapter debate these issues.

Racism Today Is Subtle, Insidious, and Systemic

Charles Quist-Adade

Charles Quist-Adade teaches at Central Michigan University and is the editor of Sankofa News, *a Canadian publication promoting multiculturalism.*

Contemporary Euro-American society has only temporarily repressed bone-chilling forms of racist evil and aggression. For example, racism in the USA has ceased to be the avowed commitment of Southern white supremacists. Now its insidious form is an unconscious habit corrupting legions of Euro-Americans, including some well-meaning ones among them.

A Different Racism

As Bernard Boxill, professor of Political and African-American Philosophy, points out, the power of the race idea to corrupt is based on a habit of deliberate disregard of what we all share with each other. "The danger to others," Boxill says, "comes when we develop a habit of repressing what we share with them and of accentuating how we differ. Such a habit develops into a habit of not seeing what we share with others, and if we do not see what we share with others, we will not see ourselves in them, and we must see ourselves in them to have sympathy for them."

Racism in Euro-America today has ceased to be the overt, crude, "in-your-face" form of racism of the past. The general consensus is that racism today is generally more subtle, sophisticated and covert. In Canada, some scholars even call it "democratic" racism, as if there could be anything democratic

Charles Quist-Adade, "What Is 'Race' and What Is 'Racism'?" *New African*, vol. 450, April 2006, pp. 46–49. Reproduced by permission.

about racism. The problem is that the benign, smiling face of racism today has made too many people of all complexions complacent. They compare what was and what is and console themselves with the usual refrain: "We have come a long way indeed."

They take tokenism—the hiring of a handful of blacks for window-dressing by white employers, for example—as improved race relations. They take a few black men and women cracking through the glass ceiling or the appointment of such figures as Colin Powell and Condoleezza Rice to powerful government positions in the US, and the success and fabulous wealth of African-American entertainers and athletes such as Michael Jackson and Michael Jordan, as clear indications of race relations having "improved vastly".

A More Harmful Racism

The fact that racism has changed its appearance and form does not make it any better. Indeed, racism in its new garbs is even more insidious and treacherous. As it is said in Ghana, the snake under the grass is more dangerous than the snake on the tree, for you can see the snake on the tree and know how to handle it—kill it or run away—but you cannot avoid the snake under the grass since it cannot be seen and, therefore, bites you without your noticing it.

The next problem is that many people tend to think that one form of racism is better than another form, or that racism in one country is better than in another. However, racism is racism. In all cases, lives are destroyed. People are harmed physically, psychologically, and emotionally. Racism in any form, quantity, or shape must not be tolerated. It is wrong for victims of racism to think they can fight this malady alone. It takes two to tango, and, as the Ghanaian philosopher and educator, Dr James Kwegyir Aggrey once said, it takes both the black and the white keys to produce harmonious music on the piano.

Also, racism affects both the victimised and the victimiser. But both the victimised and the victimiser must not only know their proper roles, they must also be conscious of, and alert to, history and changing realities of today. The French philosopher, Jean Jacques Rousseau, said that "man is born free" but is "everywhere in chains". Infants not yet smitten by the "racial bug" tend to freely relate to and play with other children across the "colour line". But the children learn too quickly the danger involved in playing and interacting with children beyond their racial pale. All too soon, the children's innate freedom is constricted with "chains" everywhere.

Learning Racism

Thandeka, an associate professor of theology and culture at the Meadville Lombard Theological School in Chicago, USA, alludes to the Rousseauian chains in her book, *Learning to Be White*. Calling the process abuse, she explains the socialisation processes children, particularly Euro-American children, go through to avoid the racial "other".

Thandeka begins with the premise that Euro-American children learn to be white and asserts that the learning process is a form of abuse. "White America's racial victim is its own child," she writes caustically, noting that most Euro-American children, for example, have not yet learned to avoid making African-American friends or to think of such people as inferior. They learn how to think of themselves as white in order to stay out of trouble with their caretakers and in the good graces of their peers or the enforcers of community racial standards. Recalling several interviews she conducted with white Americans, Thandeka concluded that Euro-American children suffered abuse—physical and psychological—from their caretakers and other significant others, because as children they were proscribed from playing with children outside their racial community.

"The child thus learns, layer by layer, to stay away from the non-white zones of its own desire.... The internal non-white zone is the killing fields of desire, the place where impulses to community with persons beyond the pale are slaughtered. The child develops antipathy toward its own forbidden feelings and to the persons who are the objects of these forbidden desires: the racial other."

Black and White

The child, and then the adult, learns how to suppress such risky feelings of camaraderie with persons beyond the community's racial pale in order to decrease the possibility of being exiled from his or her own community. My 14-year-old son, Christopher, pointed to the absurdity of race in more poignant terms in several "race-talks" with his mother and me. "This black-and-white thing doesn't make sense to me; our van is white, my pillow is black," he quibbled as we approached our next-door neighbour one afternoon. Our neighbour, a white student at Central Michigan University, shook his head in a mixture of what appeared to be astonishment and amusement: "Yeah, you're right. It doesn't to me either."

My son's comment came to us as a surprise. In an earlier conversation, he, pointing to the television set, to the video cassette recorder (VCR) and to his favourite pillow, and asked his mother: "The TV is black, the VCR is black, and my pillow is black, but I am not black, am I?"

The real issue is ability to translate prejudices and stereotypes into acts of discrimination at the personal, the state, and the systemic levels.

We were at pains to figure out the genesis of his impromptu comments, and we concluded that Christopher had eavesdropped on one of my discussions with his mother about race and racism. In my several discussions with his mother, I had stressed the silliness of people using superficial physical features such as skin colour to pigeon-hole people into the so-called races.

But "race" is more than skin colour and it transcends stereotypes and individual prejudice. All people harbour prejudices about other human groups. All people use stereotypes as rules of thumb or mental templates as they try to navigate the complex world.

Thus, stereotypes and prejudice, while universal, cut across "racial" and ethnic lines and are not the real problems. The real issue is ability to translate prejudices and stereotypes into acts of discrimination at the personal, the state, and the systemic levels.

For example, while black Britons may harbour anti-white British prejudice and stereotype all whites, and even act out their race prejudice or exhibit race animus from time to time, it is white Britons who are in the position to discriminate systematically against their black compatriots. While white British racists have a panoply of supporting institutions and agencies—the state, the judicial system, the law enforcement agencies, the media, the educational system and indeed the general culture. Black Britons do not have sufficient resources—power or otherwise—to act out their race prejudice on a systematic basis. The system simply crushes those who try.

Seeing Racism

To combat racism, the first step is to identify and remedy social policies and institutional practices that advantage some groups at the expense of others. As part of my predominantly white "Racism and Inequality" and "Racial Diversity and Media" classes in the USA, I asked my students to write a final essay about their overall impressions on racial and ethnic relations in their country. Many wrote riveting accounts about their personal upbringings and primary socialisation experiences and how these affected their view of members of the "visible" minority groups and their resolve to help end the system of racism in their country.

Many suggested that courses such as mine should be taught in grade schools, and wondered why this has not been done all this while. Almost invariably, I was also intrigued, but not surprised, by the similarities of their experiences. The majority had only fleeting encounters with "visible" minorities, and took pains to point out almost apologetically that either they or their parents were not racist. Many blamed racism on skinheads, neo-Nazis, and simply on "bad" people. Few saw themselves as part of the problem.

This year, after moving back to Canada, I gave the same assignment to my Canadian students, and, not surprisingly, their responses were no different from those of their US counterparts. In fact, their responses reflect the culture of denial and neglect in North America. For sure, to be branded a racist these days does not generate pleasant feelings, to say the least. So it is understandable that North Americans go to great lengths to deny they are racist and "part of the problem".

Responsibility for Racism

Some of my students were desperately defensive and ashamed about racism in their country and their unwitting participation in it. It is these feelings and sentiments among my students that prompted me to organise a final "debriefing lecture" at the end of each semester at which I explained to them that the problem is not of their making.

It is not the nature of whites, but the logic of the system, the rules of the game, if you will, that produce racism.

They are not responsible for the existence of racism in their country and they are not responsible for harbouring race prejudice. They were socialised, brought up, that way. However, that does not absolve them from responsibility if their actions and inactions perpetuate racism.

I explained how the socio-economic and political system works in their country to sustain, service, support, and promote the inequitable race relations. Racism exists in their country not because it is run by mean-spirited, evil-minded bigots. It is not the nature of whites, but the logic of the system, the rules of the game, if you will, that produce racism. In other words, if the tables were turned and African-Americans were the dominant ethnic/racial group in the USA, for example, they would probably act in the same way whites are acting now.

While we are products of the systems into which we are born, we are not entirely powerless.

I also reminded them that "no one is born a racist bigot". In other words, racial bigotry or racial prejudice is not genetically or biologically determined. People are products of the socio-cultural systems into which they are born. This is precisely what the French philosopher, Denis Diderot, had in mind when he wrote: "Nature has not made us evil; it is bad education, it is bad models, it is bad legislations that corrupt us."

Playing Within the System

Thus, racism is learned in the social context; it is a social construct; it is not innate. However, that does not make people slaves to the system either. People possess, and many frequently exercise, agency or free will. While we may be victims of circumstances, we are, at the same time, captains of the ships of our destinies. While we are products of the systems into which we are born, we are not entirely powerless. While we may be "victims" of our parents' upbringing, we do not remain "puppets" in our adult lives; we are capable of "unlearning" the unhealthy lessons of childhood.

This is what sociologists Peter Berger and Thomas Luckman had in mind when they proposed their theory of the duality of structure and agency, arguing that while individuals act on things, their actions take place within the context of social structures.

Allan Johnson used the game of Monopoly to illustrate this point very poignantly. Monopoly is a game of ruthless competition, a zero-sum game in which the winner takes all. According to Johnson, the point of the game is to ruin everyone else and be the only one left in at the end of the game.

A player does not even have to be a greedy person to wish to ruin his opponents in a game of Monopoly. The rules of the game, the logic of Monopoly, make players ruthless. Even an angel can be turned into the devil incarnate by playing Monopoly. But Monopoly players also have agency. They can stop simply playing Monopoly.

Thus, Johnson urges us to think of Monopoly as a social system—as something larger than ourselves that we participate in. The game of Monopoly demonstrates how "systems and people come together in a dynamic relationship that produce[s] oppression, power, and privilege". People, he explains, make social systems happen by virtue of their participation in [them].

The simple fact is that no system of social oppression can continue to exist without most people choosing to remain silent about.

If no one plays Monopoly, "it is just a box full of stuff with writing inside the cover". The problem is that "when people open it up and identify themselves as players, however, Monopoly starts to happen". In such a system, it is the actions, and indeed the inactions, of the individuals which perpetuate the system.

The Role of Silence

How do people make the systems of social injustice and in-equality, such as sexism, racism, and privilege, happen? People perpetuate systems of social injustice by adopting what Johnson calls "paths of least resistance", one of which is si-lence. To perpetuate a system of oppression and privilege, we do not have to do something consciously to support it. Just our silence is crucial enough to ensure its future; the simple fact is that no system of social oppression can continue to ex-ist without most people choosing to remain silent about it.

"If most whites spoke out about racism, it would be the first step towards a revolutionary change," Johnson declares. "Sadly," though, "the vast majority of 'good' people simply chooses the paths of least resistance and remains silent on racism, and it is easy for ethnic/racial minorities to read their silence as support for the system," Johnson concludes. Silence, as the saying goes, is golden. However, in matters of social in-justice, silence is as deadly as the sayings of these individuals, whose reactions to man's inhumanity to man in different cir-cumstances attest:

> "Throughout history, it has been the inaction of those who could have acted, the indifference of those who should have known better, the silence of the voice of justice when it mat-tered most, that has made it possible for evil to triumph"— Emperor Haile Selassie I of Ethiopia.

Racism Plays a Significant Role in Promoting Economic Inequality

Phil Martinez

Phil Martinez teaches economics at Lane Community College in Eugene, Oregon.

According to the US Census Bureau's 2005 data, net median income for white people is about $50,000 and for black families, it's close to $30,000. Whereas the median net worth of whites is $120,900, for blacks it is only $17,100. The wealth implies total assets minus liabilities.

The Wealth Gap

The Black-White wealth gap is far more indicative of the effects of racism and is much more damaging to the black community than the income gap. The wealth gap is approximately 90%, while the income gap is around 12–18%. The wealth gap is more indicative of racism because blacks were not able to own land until the late 1860s, thus, whites (especially males) have been able to accumulate, bequeath and inherit land for hundreds of years longer.

Part of the current wealth gap is directly attributable to slavery. Additionally, since the 1860s, blacks have been ghettoized and isolated on the least valuable real estate in virtually every region in the country. In the past, they were not allowed to live in certain areas through discriminatory laws, and even now are still subjected to red-lining (denial of loans and insurance on their property) and targeted for higher interest rates than whites for the same level of risk. Both of these

Phil Martinez, "The Income Ladder and Wealth Divide: A Crash Course in Economics," *Skipping Stones*, vol. 20, no. 4, September–October 2008, p. 33. Copyright © 2008 *Skipping Stones*. Reproduced by permission of the publisher and author, Phil Martinez, Instructor of Economics at Lane Community College.

claims are backed up by Federal Reserve Bank studies which undertook the research to prove there was no discrimination in banking, but were shocked to find that their own studies showed that discriminatory practices do occur.

A recent study reports that 60% of all of the foreclosed sub-prime mortgages that are currently taking place are on black-owned houses! (The study points out that these borrowers were actually targeted, knowing full well that they would, in all likelihood, be unable to make the balloon payments.)

When the black community cannot save significant amounts of wealth via real estate they are less able to afford higher education and medical care, and are unable to bequeath significant wealth to their children. Thus, low net wealth contributes to lower educational achievement, lower health indicators and generational perpetuation of poverty. It also results in lower political clout, since more wealth brings more political influence.

Income and Wealth

Since the early 1970s, one of the major trends in the U.S. economy is the growing gap between the poorest and richest sectors of the population.

Income is the flow of earnings paid for the employment of a resource. For example, wages and salaries are paid for the employment of labor; interest and dividends are paid for the employment of financial capital; and rent is paid for the employment of real estate. Income can be "turned-off," like the flow of water from a faucet, when the resource is no longer employed.

By contrast, *wealth* is a stock of owned assets. Wealth does not "flow" as income does from the employer of a resource to the resource holder. Rather, wealth "accumulates" to the owner of the stock of assets as the value of the assets appreciate. Furthermore, the assets do not need to be productive. They may be speculative since an asset can be anything that can be sold or liquidated in the market.

The most common assets (and wealth) are houses, cars, appliances, electronic equipment and jewelry. Other forms of household wealth include art collections, precious metals, heirlooms, antiques and luxury items, like boats and yachts.

The most valuable sources of wealth are business assets; such as business ownership, stocks and bonds, trademarks and patents, factories and machinery, commercial real estate and natural resources (e.g. mines, forestland and water rights).

Assets and wealth can also generate a flow of income separate from the market value (or price) of the asset itself. For example, a share of a company stock has a value, say of $89.00, and pays a dividend, say $0.05 per share.

Wealth is more important than income since it generates the ability to earn more income and thus additional wealth.

A person can have a high income and little or no wealth, such as a professional, a doctor or lawyer, putting her children through college and carrying a net debt. She may earn $120,000 but spend $130,000. Similarly, a person can have low income and still have wealth, such as a person earning minimum wage who has inherited $100,000 in stocks and decides to keep that for retirement rather than cashing it out.

Income vs. Wealth Inequality

Wealth is more important than income since it generates the ability to earn more income and thus additional wealth. As it accumulates, it eventually implies economic and even political power. Because the market rewards people based upon the value of the assets they own, the more wealth one accumulates, the less likely it is that one will fail in the market economy. The less wealth one owns, the more difficult it is to be successful in the market economy.

When the gap grows between those with higher incomes and those with lower incomes, then there is a growing gap between the rich and the poor. However, there still remains some degree of mobility between income earners. Some income earners at the low end will have their income rise over time and some at the high end will have their incomes fall over time.

However, when the gap in wealth grows, those who own more gain greater economic (and eventually political) power, while those with less wealth lose economic influence and with it, political relevance. Thus, an increasing wealth gap is potentially far more damaging to a nation's economy, democratic values and stability than an increasing income gap. Of course, over a long period of time an increasing income gap is likely to cause an increasing gap in wealth.

Racial Disparity in Prisons Is the Result of Racism

Glenn C. Loury

Glenn C. Loury is the Merton P. Stolz Professor of the Social Sciences in the Department of Economics at Brown University. He is the author of The Anatomy of Racial Inequality.

The current American prison system is a leviathan unmatched in human history. Never before has a supposedly free country denied basic liberty to so many of its citizens. In December 2006, some 2.25 million people were being held in the nearly 5,000 prisons and jails scattered across America's urban and rural landscapes. According to a 2005 report of the International Centre for Prison Studies in London, the United States—with one-twentieth of the world's population—houses one-quarter of the world's inmates. The US incarceration rate (now at 714 prisoners per 100,000 residents) is almost 40 per cent greater than the nearest competitors (the Bahamas, Belarus, and Russia). Other industrial democracies, some with significant crime problems of their own, are much less punitive: The US incarceration rate is 6.2 times that of Canada, 7.8 times that of France, and 12.3 times that of Japan. The US spends some $200 billion annually on law enforcement and corrections at all levels of Government, a fourfold increase (in constant dollars) over the past quarter century.

An Increase in Incarceration

One-third of inmates in State prisons are violent criminals, convicted of homicide, rape, or robbery. But the other two-thirds consist mainly of property and drug offenders. Inmates

Glenn C. Loury, "The New Untouchables: Crime, Punishment, and Race in America," *UN Chronicle*, vol. 44, September 2007, pp. 53–55. Adapted from "Why Are So Many Americans in Prison? Race and the Transformation of Criminal Justice," Boston Review, July/August 2007. Reproduced by permission of the author.

are disproportionately drawn from the most disadvantaged parts of society. On average, State inmates have fewer than 11 years of schooling. They are also vastly disproportionately black and brown.

Some argue that this massive increase in incarceration reflects the success of a rational public policy: faced with a compelling social problem, Americans responded by imprisoning people and succeeded in lowering crime rates. Crime rates have, indeed, fallen dramatically since reaching their peak in the early 1990s, and increased incarceration does appear to have reduced crime somewhat. But by how much? Estimates of the share of the 1990s reduction in violent crime that can be attributed to the prison boom range from 5 to 25 per cent. (That is, at most one-quarter of the recent decline in crime can be explained by the rise of imprisonment.) Whatever the number, analysts of all political stripes now agree that we have long ago entered the zone of diminishing returns.

A black male resident of the state of California is more likely to go to a state prison than a state college.

Imprisonment rates have continued to rise while crime rates have fallen for the simple reason that US criminal justice policy has become much more punitive. The nation has made a collective decision to punish offenders more severely. Thus, between 1980 and 2001, the chances of someone being arrested in response to a criminal complaint stayed constant, at just under 50 per cent. But, over this same period, the likelihood that an arrest would result in imprisonment more than doubled, from 13 to 28 per cent. As a result, the incarceration rate for violent crime almost tripled, despite a sharp decline in the level of violence. Incarceration rates for nonviolent and drug offenses increased at an even faster pace: between 1980 and 1997 the number of people imprisoned for nonviolent offenses tripled, and the number incarcerated for drug offenses increased elevenfold.

Racial Disparity in Prison

To be sure, in the United States, as in any society, public order is maintained by the threat and use of force. We enjoy our good lives in part because we are shielded by the forces of law and order, which keep the unruly at bay. Yet in this society, to a degree virtually unmatched in any other, those bearing the brunt of law enforcement belong in vastly disproportionate numbers to historically marginalized racial groups. Crime and punishment in America has a color. The extent of racial disparity in imprisonment rates is greater than in any other major arena of American social life: At eight to one, the black-white ratio of incarceration rates dwarfs the two-to-one ratio of unemployment rates, the three-to-one ratio of non-marital child-bearing, the two-to-one ratio of infant-mortality rates, and one-to-five ratio of net worth. While three out of 200 young white men were incarcerated in 2000, the rate for young black males was one in nine. A black male resident of the state of California is more likely to go to a state prison than a state college.

Race was a central factor influencing the evolution of American social policy in the last third of the twentieth century.

The scandalous truth is that the police and penal apparatus are now the primary contact between adult black American men and the American State. Among black male high-school dropouts aged 20 to 40, a third were locked up on any given day in 2000, fewer than three per cent belonged to a union, and less than one quarter were enrolled in any kind of social program. Coercion is the most salient meaning of government for these young men. Sociologist Bruce Western estimates that nearly 60 per cent of black male dropouts born between 1965 and 1969 were sent to prison on a felony conviction at least once before they reached the age of 35.

This punitive turn in the nation's social policy—intimately connected with public rhetoric about responsibility, dependency, social hygiene, and the reclamation of public order—can be fully grasped only when viewed against the backdrop of America's often ugly and violent racial history. An historical resonance between the stigma of race and the stigma of imprisonment serves to keep alive in US public culture the subordinating social meanings that have always been associated with blackness. The subtle and not-so-subtle consequences of America's history of race relations helps to explain why the US is exceptional among democratic industrial societies in the severity and extent of its punitive policy and in the paucity of its social-welfare institutions. Race was a central factor influencing the evolution of American social policy in the last third of the twentieth century.

After the Civil Rights Movement

The political scientist Vesla Mae Weaver, in a recently completed dissertation, examines policy history, public opinion, and media processes in an attempt to understand the role of race in this historic transformation of criminal justice. She argues—persuasively, I think—that the punitive turn represented a political response to the success of the civil-rights movement. Weaver describes a process of "frontlash" in which opponents of the civil-rights revolution sought to regain the upper hand by shifting to a new issue. Rather than reacting directly to civil-rights developments, and thus continuing to fight a battle they had lost, those opponents shifted attention from a political demand for racial equality to a seemingly race-neutral concern over crime:

Once the clutch of Jim Crow had loosened, opponents of civil rights shifted the "locus of attack" by injecting crime onto the agenda. Through the process of frontlash, rivals of civil rights progress defined racial discord as criminal and argued that crime legislation would be a panacea to racial unrest. This strategy both imbued crime with race and depoliticized racial struggle, a formula which foreclosed earlier "root causes" alternatives. Fusing anxiety about crime to anxiety over racial change and riots, civil rights and racial disorder—initially defined as a problem of minority disenfranchisement—were defined as a crime problem, which helped shift debate from social reform to punishment.

So consider the nearly 60 per cent of black male high-school dropouts born in the late 1960s who are imprisoned before their 40th year. While locked up, these felons are stigmatized; their links to family disrupted; their opportunities for work diminished; their voting rights may be permanently revoked. They suffer civic excommunication. America's zeal for social discipline consigns these men to a permanent nether caste. And yet, since these men—whatever their shortcomings—have emotional needs, including the need to be fathers, lovers and husbands, we are creating a situation where the children of this nether caste are likely to join a new generation of untouchables. This cycle will continue so long as incarceration is viewed as the primary path to social hygiene.

One cannot reckon the world-historic American prison build-up over the past 35 years without calculating the enormous costs imposed upon the persons imprisoned, their families, and their communities. This is a question of social morality, not social hygiene. Nor can social science tell us how much additional cost borne by the offending class is justified in order to obtain a given increment of security for property or peace of mind for the rest of us. These questions about the nature of the American State and its relationship to its people transcend the categories of benefits and costs.

Us and Them

Yet the discourse surrounding punishment policy invariably discounts the humanity of the thieves, drug sellers, prostitutes, rapists, and, yes, those whom the State puts to death. It gives insufficient weight to the welfare, to the humanity, of those who are knitted together with offenders in webs of social and psychic affiliation. What is more, institutional arrangements for dealing with criminal offenders in the United States have evolved to serve expressive as well as instrumental ends. We wanted to "send a message," and have done so with a vengeance. In the process, we have created not only facts, but also constructed a national narrative of blame. We have created scapegoats and assuaged our fears. We have met the enemy, and the enemy is them, the others.

This situation raises a moral problem that we Americans cannot avoid.

Incarceration keeps them away from us. The sociologist David Garland writes: "The prison is used today as a kind of reservation, a quarantine zone in which purportedly dangerous individuals are segregated in the name of public safety." This situation is morally problematic in the extreme. We Americans have chosen to invest in human punishment, but not in human development. Our society creates crime-promoting conditions in our sprawling urban ghettos, and then acts out rituals of punishment against them as some awful form of human sacrifice. We law-abiding, middle-class Americans have, through our elected representatives, made decisions about social policy that benefit us, created from a system of suffering, rooted in State violence.

This situation raises a moral problem that we Americans cannot avoid. We cannot pretend that there are more important problems in our society—unless we are also prepared to say that we have turned our backs on the ideal of equality for all citizens and abandoned the principles of justice. We ought to be asking ourselves the fundamental question: What are our obligations to our fellow citizens—even those who break our laws?

A Thought Experiment

To aid in thinking about the moral dimensions of the current situation, I wish to suggest a thought-experiment: Let us imagine, in the spirit of the political philosopher, John Rawls, that any one of us could occupy any rank in the social hierarchy. Let me be more concrete: Imagine that you could be born a black American male outcast shuffling between prison and the labor market on his way to an early death to the chorus of *nigger* or *criminal* or *dummy*. What social rules would we pick if we actually thought that they could be us? If any one of us had a real chance of being one of those faces looking up from the bottom of the well—of being the least among us—then how would we talk publicly about those who break our laws? What would we do with juveniles who go awry, who roam the streets with guns and sometimes commit acts of violence? What weight would we give to various elements in the deterrence-retribution-incapacitation-rehabilitation calculus, if we thought that calculus could end up being applied to our own children, or to us? How would we apportion blame and affix responsibility for the cultural and social pathologies evident in some quarters of our society if we envisioned that we ourselves might well have been born into the social margins where such pathology flourishes? I expect that we would still pick some set of punishment institutions to contain bad behavior and protect society. But wouldn't we pick arrangements that respected the humanity of each individual and of those they are connected to through bonds of social and psychic affiliation?

Moreover, continuing with the thought-experiment, wouldn't we also recognize a kind of social responsibility, even for the wrongful acts freely chosen by individuals? This is not to argue that people commit crimes because they have no choices, or that in this sense the "root causes" of crime are social; individuals always have choices. My point is that society at large is implicated in an individual's choices because we have acquiesced in—perhaps actively supported, through our taxes and votes, words and deeds—social arrangements that work to our benefit yet to that person's detriment. These discriminatory arrangements shape his consciousness and sense of identity in such a way that the choices he makes, which we may condemn, are nevertheless compelling to him—an entirely understandable response to circumstance. Closed and bounded social structures—like racially homogeneous urban ghettos—create contexts where "pathological" and "dysfunctional" cultural forms emerge; but these forms are neither intrinsic to the people caught in these structures nor independent of the behavior of people who stand outside them.

Mass incarceration has now become a principal vehicle for the reproduction of racial hierarchy in US society.

Our Collective Responsibility

When we hold a person responsible for his or her conduct—by establishing laws, investing in their enforcement, and consigning some persons to prison—we need also to think about whether we have done our share in ensuring that each person faces a decent set of opportunities for a good life. We need to ask whether we as a society have fulfilled our collective responsibility to ensure fair conditions for each person—for each life that might turn out to be our life. And what American can honestly say that we now have laws and policies that we would endorse if we did not know our own situation and genuinely considered the possibility that we might be the least advantaged?

Too many Americans fail to see that, because of the paucity of our social welfare institutions, we as a society are collectively responsible for creating conditions that spawn the wrongful acts of individual persons. As a result, the enormous racial disparity in the imposition of social exclusion, civic excommunication, and lifelong disgrace has come to seem legitimate. We shift all the responsibility onto their shoulders, only by irresponsibly—indeed, immorally—denying our own. And yet this entire dynamic has its roots in past unjust acts that were perpetrated on the basis of race.

Producing a racially defined nether caste through the ostensibly neutral application of law should be profoundly offensive to our ethical sensibilities—to the principles we proudly assert as our own—a nation conceived in liberty and dedicated to the proposition that all persons are created equal. Mass incarceration has now become a principal vehicle for the reproduction of racial hierarchy in US society. Our country's policymakers need to do something about it. And all of us Americans are ultimately responsible for making sure that they do.

Institutional Racism Is an Invention to Stifle Dissent

Roger Scruton

Roger Scruton is a writer and philosopher who is research professor for the Institute for the Psychological Sciences. He is author of A Political Philosophy.

When John Stuart Mill gave his famous defense of free opinion in *On Liberty*, he was careful to point out that errors are not only inevitable, they are also beneficial, provided we are able to confess to them. As he put it: "the peculiar evil of silencing the expression of an opinion is, that it is robbing the human race; posterity as well as the existing generation; those who dissent from the opinion, still more than those who hold it. If the opinion is right, they are deprived of the opportunity of exchanging error for truth; if wrong, they lose, what is almost as great a benefit, the clearer perception and livelier impression of truth, produced by its collision with error." That elegant way of saying that we learn from our mistakes has the merit of showing *why* we learn from them and *how*. The greatest mistake in politics was that made by [Russian revolutionary leader Vladimir] Lenin, when he set about destroying the institutions in which opposition could express itself: the mistake of making it impossible to perceive one's own mistakes. It took 70 years for the resulting machine [communism] without feedback to crash—but 60 million people had to die before it did so.

Discouraging Dissent

However, people have not learned the lesson of that, or of any other experience of censorship. Movements to silence opinion, or to enforce orthodoxy, are almost as strong in a democratic

Roger Scruton, "Truth and Self-Censorship," *The American Spectator*, vol. 40, no. 10, December 2007, pp. 62–64. Copyright © 2007 *The American Spectator*. Reproduced by permission.

culture as they are in a totalitarian tyranny. Of course, a democratic society does not dispose of the same threats and punishments. It can enforce orthodoxies only through marginalizing those who defy them. But such methods can be equally effective, since society begins from agreement and usually ends there. That is why conversations with strangers start with remarks about the weather: they are remarks guaranteed to elicit agreement, and so to establish a bond. Imagine a society in which all conversations began with a declaration of political convictions: it would be a society on the brink of civil war.

Mill's observation remains valid. If we discourage dissent, we perpetuate error. What Mill did not sufficiently emphasize, however, is that the discouraging of dissent is always profoundly motivated. And it is motivated, as a rule, by the knowledge of error. It is precisely when people have invested in errors that they are afraid of the truth, and therefore eager to silence those who proclaim it. This can be witnessed in all the areas of policy where debate has been frozen, and it is instructive to study two salient examples.

Those who suggest that welfare benefits might be the cause of the problem, rather than the solution to it, risk having their heads bitten off.

Censorship About Race

One, of great concern to Americans, is the issue of the behavior and prospects of African Americans. The official view, endorsed by the liberal media and the academic establishment, is that the poor performance of African-American children in school and college, the disproportionate rates of crime and delinquency among African-American adolescents, and the breakdown of the African-American family are all the long-term effect of slavery and racial discrimination. The remedy is to reverse the process whereby blacks were reduced to second-class citizens, and this we can do through subsidies, welfare benefits, and reverse discrimination.

We all know that it is dangerous to dissent from that orthodoxy. Yet it simply cannot be true. Right up until the 1950s, blacks, who were struggling against undeniable prejudice and discrimination and were economically disadvantaged as a result, held together as families, often set a model of good behavior, and were hardly more disposed to crime than their white contemporaries. Yet today, 40 years on from the Civil Rights Act, the picture is very different—horrifyingly so—with 70 percent of black children born out of wedlock, escalating crime rates, and a steep relative decline in school performance. The official explanation of such facts just *has* to be wrong. However, a vast investment has been made in that official explanation, which defines a comfortable whitewash for the liberal conscience, as well as a lucrative source of income for the rent-seekers of the social services. Those who suggest that welfare benefits might be the cause of the problem, rather than the solution to it, risk having their heads bitten off, and will certainly find themselves marginalized in any academic community.

Of course, that suggestion might be wrong, and I am not committing myself to its truth—although it is common sense to suggest that, if you reward bad behavior, then bad behavior will increase. The point is that, if we are not prepared to consider such an argument, we are merely protecting as orthodoxy a belief whose falsehood may be the root cause of the problem.

So great is the censorship surrounding this and the related issue of race that we are beginning to witness a kind of "preemptive cringe" on the part of the liberal conscience whenever the issue is remotely likely to be raised. People have witnessed the punishments inflicted on the unorthodox, who are accused of racism or (in the case of [conservative commentator] Thomas Sowell) "Uncle-Tomism" and duly anathematized. A political career will not survive this punishment, nor as a rule will a career in journalism or the academy. The safest thing, when the issue of black-white relations is in the offing, is to declare your orthodoxy in the loudest possible terms, maybe attacking, if you can, the nearest person at whom the charge of racism might be leveled, however implausibly. This we witnessed in the singularly distressing case of the Duke lacrosse team, members of which were falsely accused of rape by a black stripper, in a case that threatened to put the whole university on show as a white supremacist enclave. As soon as the trial was announced 88 faculty members joined the calumny, adding their signatures to a letter whose main purpose was less the pursuit of justice than the urgent need to declare the impeccable orthodoxy of those who had rushed to sign it.

Another Example of Censorship

The same dynamic can be witnessed in the matter of homosexuality, the official view of which is that it is neither a perversion nor a disorder, but an "orientation" that has as much claim to social endorsement as the heterosexual alternative. The suggestions that homosexual desire is different in kind from heterosexual desire, that it has adverse medical, social, or psychological consequences, that it poses a threat to children or to new recruits that is not posed by the traditional alternative—all such suggestions are anathema. Of course, the suggestions may be wrong. But if any one of them is right, then the orthodoxy upon which the fabric of "gay rights" has come to rest will begin to crumble. And far too much has been invested in the received opinion to permit it to be questioned. Look at the academic literature on homosexuality and you won't find a whisper of disapproval, and the disturbing medical and social statistics are glossed over as though they are barely worth a mention. [Philosopher Michel] Foucault's *History of Sexuality*, according to which all "problematization" of the sexual act merely reflects the interests of those with social power and has no other source of validity, is widely regarded as the supremely authoritative text, to deviate from which is to lose credibility, respectability, and, in the extreme case, tenure.

Charges of Racism and Homophobia

Orthodoxies emerge from indignation: People, rightly protesting against racial prejudice, expressed their championship of American blacks in angry ways. And others immediately responded with pre-emptive excuses. The best way to protect yourself, when others are making angry accusations, is to agree with the accuser and deflect the accusation from yourself by accusing a third party. You look around for the *real* racist; you invent a concealed social evil, *institutional racism*, and dedicate yourself to its eradication. You become first in the ranks of name-callers and search for the slightest evidence of dissent in order to seize the opportunity to show that you too are angry, you too are on the side of the victim, you too are prepared to go to the barricades in the cause and to denounce the culprits. The fact that you are behaving like a coward, taking the softest option and in the course of it committing the greatest injustice to a new class of victim—namely the one whom you are prepared to ruin rather than listen to—is a fact that you fail to notice. For if you did notice it, you would also notice just how far you had gone down the path of error.

Maybe we must resign ourselves to living in a censored environment.

Likewise, those who first protested against the unjust treatment of homosexuals in our society expressed themselves with understandable indignation. Immediately the same pre-emptive spasm of exculpation arose. And in order that the defense mechanism should be complete, people hit on the concept of "homophobia," in order to express their militant orthodoxy and their determination to root out the real social evil. The concept is vague, without boundaries: Almost anybody can be pushed into its ring of fire. Hence the slightest divergence from orthodoxy can be singled out and punished, by the one who wishes to show his impeccable liberal credentials. As a result the academy today is full of courses dedicated to the normalization of homosexuality, as a lifestyle and a culture. But nowhere, to my knowledge, is there a department of psychology, of medicine, still less of philosophy or literature, where the truth about homosexuality and about its social, psychological, and medical consequences is impartially studied.

\Does this matter? Well, I have given two cases where it seems to me that the growing censoriousness of modern democracies has mattered greatly, and will go on to matter even more, as errors become too deeply embedded to be corrected. We used to think that academies had the purpose of protecting free enquiry, however shocking or disturbing its results, precisely so that errors propagated in the surrounding culture will eventually be brought to book and eliminated. But this no longer happens. For it is in the academy that orthodoxies now arise, taking advantage of the new forms of scholarship, the easily invented intellectual "disciplines" designed to protect rather than to examine a prejudice, and the career structure in which dissent can be marked down as intellectual incompetence. Maybe the Internet will help us—but again, I doubt it, having witnessed the ease in which orthodoxies are propagated through those supposedly impartial sources like Wikipedia, which are not impartial at all, but merely hostage to majority opinion, and never more hostage than when the majority is wrong. Maybe we must resign ourselves to living in a censored environment, and look for those "little platoons" of free inquiry which exist among friends, and in which the only settled agreement is the agreement to differ.

Racism Is Not the Most Significant Factor in Economic Inequality

Duncan Currie

Duncan Currie is a reporter for The Weekly Standard *magazine.*

I'll say this for Barack Obama's big speech [on March 18, 2008]: It is still being analyzed [more than a week later], and it will be analyzed more in the weeks and months ahead. Senator Obama went beyond the controversy over his former pastor, Reverend Jeremiah Wright, and delivered a sweeping address on the recent history of U.S. race relations. But he gave short shrift to an issue that is inseparable from racial inequality: the issue of out-of-wedlock births.

Before and After the Civil Rights Act

"So many of the disparities that exist in the African-American community today can be directly traced to inequalities passed on from an earlier generation that suffered under the brutal legacy of slavery and Jim Crow," Obama said. He did acknowledge that welfare policies "may" have hurt black families. But he affirmed with certainty that "a lack of economic opportunity among black men, and the shame and frustration that came from not being able to provide for one's family, contributed to the erosion of black families."

That's true. But it's also true that African-American families were much more intact in the decades *before* the Civil Rights Act than they were in the decades after it. In 1963, according to the famous Department of Labor report issued by

Daniel Patrick Moynihan two years later, the out-of-wedlock birth rate among blacks was 23.6 percent while the rate among whites was only 3.07 percent. By 2005, according to the National Center for Health Statistics, the out-of-wedlock birth rate among non-Hispanic whites had jumped to 25.3 percent and the rate among non-Hispanic blacks stood at nearly 70 percent.

In other words, the black out-of-wedlock birth rate was lower in 1963—on the eve of the Civil Rights Act, when Jim Crow policies were still an ugly reality in the American South and white racism was far more widespread than it is today—than the non-Hispanic white rate was in 2005. While Moynihan was right to raise the alarm, the numbers show that African-American families proved remarkably durable through decades of repression and racism following Reconstruction. The most severe "erosion of black families" in the 20th century occurred in the years *after* the civil rights movement reached its apotheosis, when black economic opportunities were expanding rapidly. What explains that?

Out-of-Wedlock Birth Rates and Poverty

Broadly speaking, American society underwent a cultural revolution in the late 1960s and early 1970s. Since then, out-of-wedlock birth rates among both blacks and whites have shot upward. But blacks were starting from a much higher base, and the spike among blacks was more precipitous than the spike among whites. As Heritage Foundation scholar Robert Rector has noted, the black out-of-wedlock birth rate ballooned from less than 25 percent in the early 1960s to 49 percent in 1975 and to 70 percent in 1995. The white rate increased from less than 5 percent in the early 1960s to 25 percent in 2005.

The connection between family breakdown and child poverty is well established. In a 1991 *American Sociological Review* article, David J. Eggebeen and Daniel T. Lichter estimated that if black family composition had remained constant from 1960 to 1988, the black child poverty rate in 1988 would have been 28.4 percent instead of 45.6 percent. If black family composition had remained constant from 1980 to 1988, Eggebeen and Lichter said, the black child poverty rate in 1988 would have been 40 percent instead of 45.6 percent.

"This implies that changing black family structure in the 1980s accounted for roughly 65 percent of the increase in official poverty among black children," they noted. "Black family shifts in the 1980s also accounted for 51 percent of the increase in deep poverty, and about 90 percent of the growth in relative child poverty." Family breakdown also had an intensifying effect on the child poverty rates of whites, but it "had a much greater effect on the child poverty rates of blacks."

Today it is culture—not racism or a dearth of economic opportunities—that poses the biggest threat to black family structures, and thus to black progress.

In 1960, according to the Eggebeen-Lichter analysis, racial disparities in child poverty "had very little to do with racial differences in family structure." Yet by 1988, this was no longer true. "Racial differences in child poverty cannot be explained by racial differences in family structure alone," they wrote. "At the same time, the changing family structure among black and white children has clearly *exacerbated* long-standing racial differences in child poverty. Indeed, in the absence of widening racial differences in family structure, the 1960–1988 period would have brought substantial *convergence* in racial differences in official, deep, and relative child poverty."

The Effect of Marriage

More recently, a 2002 study by Rector and two of his Heritage colleagues concluded that "if marriage were restored to 1960 levels," the black child poverty rate "would fall by nearly a third." A separate 2002 study by Urban Institute economist Robert Lerman, which relied on data from the Survey of Income and Program Participation, found that "married couple households were much more likely to avoid poverty than all other types of households," and that "the apparent gains from marriage are particularly high among black households."

Due to America's racial history, blacks were uniquely vulnerable to the debilitating cultural trends of the post-1960s era and to the perverse incentives created by the federal welfare system. And indeed, today it is culture—not racism or a dearth of economic opportunities—that poses the biggest threat to black family structures, and thus to black progress. Any serious discussion of race must address that reality.

Disparity in Prison Populations Is Not the Result of Racism

Stuart Taylor Jr.

Stuart Taylor Jr. is a nonresident senior fellow of governance studies at the Brookings Institution, a Newsweek *contributing editor, and a columnist for the* National Journal.

It is regrettable that the legend of the "Jena Six" has for many become the leading symbol of the grave injustices to African-Americans that pervade our nation's penal system. The legend is partly false. And the notion that racism is the main reason for the injustices to hundreds of thousands of black defendants around the nation is entirely false.

To be sure, there is still too much racism among prosecutors, judges, and jurors. But this is far less widespread and virulent, even in Jena, La., than Al Sharpton and Jesse Jackson—the media-anointed (albeit, repeatedly discredited) African-American "leaders"—like to pretend. There are still too many unwarranted prosecutions of innocent minority (and other) defendants, as detailed in my August 4 column, "Innocents in Prison." But the vast majority of those prosecuted are guilty, as may prove to be the case with some or all of the Jena Six.

Rather, the heart of the racial injustice in our penal system is the grossly excessive punishment of hundreds of thousands of nonviolent, disproportionately black offenders whose long prison terms ruin countless lives and turn many who could have become productive citizens into career criminals.

The Supreme Court heard two cases on October 2 that focus on a relatively small piece of this problem: how much discretion federal district judges have to depart from federal sentencing guidelines that provide savagely severe prison terms for small-time drug offenders, among others. The most savage penalties of all are for people—overwhelmingly, black people—caught with fairly small amounts of crack cocaine.

The notion that racism is the main reason for the injustices to hundreds of thousands of black defendants around the nation is entirely false.

But the justices, hemmed in by wrong-headed mandatory sentencing laws, are merely rearranging deck chairs on the *Titanic*, no matter how they rule. Nothing that the Court will ever do could make much of a dent in the overly punitive regime that has sent the number of prisoners in this country soaring to 2.2 million, more than in any other nation. This represents more than a *sixfold* increase in the number of incarcerated Americans since 1970, when it was 330,000. More than 40 percent of these prisoners are black. And according to a recent study by the nonprofit Sentencing Project, 500,000 of the 2.2 million are locked up for drug crimes, and a majority of the convicted drug prisoners have no history of violence or high-level drug-selling.

Such are the fruits of decades of tough-on-crime posturing by politicians. Now a bipartisan group in Congress is pushing to alleviate some of the most excessive penalties, especially in crack cases. This is a small blessing. But the proposed tinkering is a far cry from the enormous policy changes needed. A more hopeful sign was a Joint Economic Committee hearing set by Jim Webb, for October 4 titled "Mass Incarceration in the United States: At What Cost?"

But in the end, only a vast change of attitude on the part of the voters, and in turn among the state and federal officials they elect, could return sanity to the system.

With our bloated incarceration rates, especially for non-violent drug crimes, "the system takes men with limited education and job skills and stigmatizes them in a way that makes it hard for them to find jobs, slashes their wages when they do find them, and brands them as bad future spouses," as Christopher Shea wrote in a September 23 column in *The Boston Globe.* "The effects of imprisonment ripple out from prisoners, breaking up families and further impoverishing neighborhoods, creating the conditions for more crime down the road."

The main reason that an overly punitive system has such a severe effect on black men is that they commit hugely disproportionate numbers of crimes.

Our penal system visits these dire consequences on a staggeringly high percentage of the African-American population. More than 22 percent of all black men in their early 30s and more than half of the subset who dropped out of high school have spent time behind bars. These percentages are far higher than they were during the worst era of American apartheid.

Is this situation the fault of white racism? Well, the main reason that an overly punitive system has such a severe effect on black men is that they commit hugely disproportionate numbers of crimes. As *The Economist* points out, "Young black men are seven times more likely to be jailed than whites, but they are also seven times more likely to murder someone, and their victims are usually black."

The absurdly excessive penalties for possessing or selling crack cocaine could be seen as evidence that many white voters and legislators are subconsciously more willing to throw away the lives of small-time black offenders than small-time white offenders. You can call that racism, but only by stretching the word. Especially since the most severe crack cocaine sentences of all had strong support in the Congressional Black Caucus when they were adopted in 1986 and thereafter. Black officials hoped that long prison terms would quiet the "crack wars" that were then consuming inner cities. The Clinton administration also supported these laws.

Orlando Patterson, the noted African-American sociology professor at Harvard, put his finger on the main source of racial injustice in a September 30 *New York Times* op-ed:

Focusing mainly on the residue of racism is a distraction from the far bigger problem of over-punishment.

"This virtual gulag of racial incarceration [reflects] a law enforcement system that unfairly focuses on drug offenses and other crimes more likely to be committed by blacks, combined with draconian mandatory sentencing and an absurdly counterproductive retreat from rehabilitation [of] offenders. [This system] simply makes hardened criminals of nonviolent drug offenders and spits out angry men who are unemployable, unreformable, and unmarriageable."

In short, focusing mainly on the residue of racism is a distraction from the far bigger problem of over-punishment. It is also a distraction from understanding why African-American crime rates are so high.

The reason, Patterson says, is "something that has been swept under the rug for too long in black America: the crisis in relations between men and women of all classes and, as a result, the catastrophic state of black family life, especially among the poor. . . . The resulting absence of fathers—some 70 percent of black babies are born to single mothers—is undoubtedly a major cause of youth delinquency."

This is not to deny that the Jena case involved a clear injustice to identifiable African-Americans. Nor is it necessarily to deny the (debatable, in my view) assertions that Jena school authorities and/or the local district attorney used a racial double standard favoring white students over blacks.

The clear injustice was the initial use of a grossly excessive charge—attempted second-degree murder—that could have doomed five of the Jena Six to long prison terms for ganging up on Justin Barker, a white student who was neither attacked with a deadly weapon nor seriously injured. Indeed, after a much-needed outcry the charges were reduced to aggravated second-degree battery.

The 10,000 to 20,000 African-Americans who traveled to Jena from all over the country on September 20 also protested that the authorities allowed white students who hung nooses on a tree and got into fights to escape serious punishment, while throwing the book at the blacks who attacked Justin Barker.

But even if that's true, the Jena case is far from being the civil-rights morality play scripted by Sharpton, Jackson, and some in the media. Contrary to their spin, the December 4, 2006, gang attack on Barker was no "schoolyard fight." Nor was it a direct response to the deplorable (but noncriminal) hanging of nooses on a schoolyard tree by *other* white students *more than three months earlier.*

In fact, then-16-year-old Mychal Bell, who had been arrested four times for alleged violent offenses, is accused of knocking Barker unconscious in an unprovoked, blindside attack. Then, the charges say, all of the Jena Six (or seven, as it now appears) stomped the prostrate victim until an uninvolved student intervened. Barker was briefly hospitalized with a concussion and multiple bruises.

"In American law," as James Kirchick wrote in the gay online magazine *Advocate.com,* "you are not entitled to beat a defenseless and innocent person because someone with the same skin color as that person offended you months earlier."

Imagine for a moment that the races of the Jena students had been reversed, and that six whites had ganged up on a lone black student. I suspect that there might have been an even bigger Sharpton-Jackson-led protest. But instead of attacking the prosecutor for being too hard on the black thugs who beat up a solitary victim, the protesters would have been demanding that the white thugs be imprisoned for "hate crimes." And so would some of the same media commentators who have decried the prosecutions of the Jena Six.

They would do better to turn their fire on the real reasons why so many African-Americans end up in prison: cruel sentencing laws, crummy education, and weak families.

Is Affirmative Action Effective Against Racism?

Affirmative Action: An Overview

Michael Bérubé

Michael Bérubé is the Paterno Professor in English Literature and Science, Technology, and Society at Pennsylvania State University.

Affirmative action, in theory, is a matter of distributive justice, which is why liberals and progressives tend to look benevolently on it while conservatives and libertarians consider it a travesty. But in practice, does it actually advance the cause of justice in America? In some respects it has attempted to remedy the long-term effects of slavery and racial segregation; then again, programs that benefit women and recent immigrants cannot be defended on those grounds. Is it supposed to enhance "diversity" in colleges, professional schools and workplaces, or is it more specifically a set of programs for enhancing the class mobility of people who are structurally disadvantaged from birth? How can we decide whether affirmative action has been successful—and how can we decide whether affirmative action could ever be so successful as to become obsolete?

Arguments For and Against

Advocates of affirmative action have three arguments at their disposal: It is a corrective for past inequality and oppression; it is a corrective for present inequality, much of which derives from past inequality and oppression; and diversity in the classroom or the workplace is not only a positive good in itself but conducive to greater social goods (a more capable global workforce and a more cosmopolitan environment in which

Michael Bérubé, "And Justice for All," *The Nation*, vol. 280, no. 3, January 24, 2005, p. 27. Copyright © 2005 by The Nation Magazine/The Nation Company, Inc. Reproduced by permission.

people engage with others of different backgrounds and beliefs). Critics of affirmative action, for their part, have insisted that it is unfair to people who have never practiced race or gender discrimination; that it is counterproductive insofar as it damages the self-esteem of its beneficiaries and the public trust of institutions that practice it; and that it has deleterious consequences for society at large, because it promotes the unqualified and the incompetent over the talented and industrious.

Affirmative action in college admissions has been problematic, sometimes rewarding well-to-do immigrants over poor African-American applicants—except that all the other alternatives, like offering admission to the top 10 or 20 percent of high school graduates in a state, seem to be even worse, admitting badly underprepared kids from the top tiers of impoverished urban and rural schools while keeping out talented students who don't make their school's talented tenth. In the workplace, affirmative action has been checkered by fraud and confounded by the indeterminacy of racial identities—and yet it's so popular as to constitute business as usual for American big business, as evidenced by the sixty-eight Fortune 500 corporations, twenty-nine former high-ranking military leaders and twenty-eight broadcast media companies and organizations that filed amicus briefs in support of the University of Michigan's affirmative action programs in the recent Supreme Court cases of *Gratz v. Bollinger* and *Grutter v. Bollinger* (2003).

In some respects [affirmative action] has attempted to remedy the long-term effects of slavery and racial segregation.

The thorny legal and political issues affirmative action raises are made still more complex by the fact that affirmative action is inevitably recursive: The extent to which it works in practice depends considerably on our interpretations of it. Administrators and organizations that oppose it tend to be quite bad at implementing it; likewise, female and minority students and employees who are told that they are taking the places of more qualified applicants tend to doubt themselves and perform less capably than women and minorities who are told that they have every right to be right where they are. . . .

So what do Americans really think of affirmative action? It depends on how you pose the question. In 2003, [Terry] Anderson reports [in the *Pursuit of Fairness*], "opinion polls found that Americans approved 2 to 1 of 'programs designed to increase the number of black and minority students'; the same people disapproved 3 to 1 of 'giving preferential treatment' to minorities and that included a *majority* of minority respondents." At the end of two generations' debate about racial and social justice, it would seem, Americans emphatically approve of affirmative action programs, even as they passionately oppose any race or gender "preferences" that would make affirmative action programs work.

America's History

Thomas Sowell, a prominent black conservative sociologist at the Hoover Institution, has been arguing against affirmative action for more than thirty years, and in *Affirmative Action Around the World* , a couple of Sowell's arguments are incontrovertible. He's right, for example, that "no historic sufferings of blacks in the United States can justify preferential benefits to white women or to recently arrived immigrants from Asia or Latin America who happen to be non-white, but whose ancestors obviously never suffered any discrimination in the United States." He cites the federal largesse showered upon the Fanjul family of Cuban émigrés, who possess "a fortune exceeding $500 million" (but then so does Anderson, in the course of acknowledging that affirmative action, like any system, can be gamed by unscrupulous players). And Sowell is right that the implementation of affirmative action in the United States since the mid-1960s has gone well beyond the race-neutral language of the Civil Rights Act and LBJ's [President Lyndon B. Johnson's] executive order 11246.

There's no denying that the group polarization that preceded and produced affirmative action—segregation, Jim Crow, lynching—has been deadly in its effects.

But Sowell is not content with merely plausible arguments; he wants to insist, by way of surveys of India, Malaysia, Sri Lanka and Nigeria, that "quotas and preferences" can lead to mass murder and civil war, as when Sri Lankan Sinhalese attempted to marginalize the dominant Sri Lankan Tamils by means of punitive quotas, and Tamils fought back with protests and guerrilla war, or when Malays instituted such a draconian set of "racial preferences" as to provoke an exodus of high-skilled Chinese from Malaysia. At times Sowell has the honesty to admit that he has no idea whether these "affirmative action" programs are the cause of all the civil unrest he documents: "If it is difficult to isolate the effects of preferences and quotas, as such, on Nigeria's troubled history, it is much clearer that the group polarization which preceded and produced the preferences and quotas has been deadly in its effects." But this is like saying that it's not clear whether we should attribute "race-related violence" in the United States to affirmative action or to slavery and segregation: While it's difficult to isolate the impact of affirmative action on America's troubled history, there's no denying that the group polarization that preceded and produced affirmative action—segregation, Jim Crow, lynching—has been deadly in its effects.

A Question of Life and Death

Yet when Sowell finally gets to discussing the United States, it turns out that affirmative-action-inspired mass murder and civil war are the least of our worries. Never mind that the quota systems of Nigeria and Malaysia have never been enacted here; never mind that while India has extended its terribly amorphous category of "backward classes," the United States has backed away from controversial practices like set-asides and race-norming. For Sowell, affirmative action in America is literally a question of life and death, as illustrated by the case of Patrick Chavis, a black man admitted to the medical school of the University of California, Davis, the same school that rejected Allan Bakke. For years, the liberal affirmative action establishment touted Chavis, as Sowell notes: "The Lawyers Committee for Civil Rights made the usual comparison between Chavis and Bakke—to Chavis' advantage—in 1997, just two weeks before the Medical Board of California suspended Chavis' license to practice medicine in the wake of a suspicions death of one of his patients."

For Sowell, Chavis clinches the argument: "the role of academic institutions is not to play God in judging individual souls. It is, among other things, to see that people like Patrick Chavis do not end up with scalpels in their hands and 'M.D.' after their names to lure unsuspecting patients to their deaths." And Chavis is "not an isolated example"; on the contrary, Chavises have infected the system at every level, corrupting American meritocracy and placing us all at risk:

> In other fields as well, it is the ignored third parties who have the biggest stake in what institutions of higher learning do and how well they do it. Applicants for engineering schools do not have nearly as large a stake as those millions of other people whose lives depend on the quality of the engineering that goes into the bridges they drive across or the planes they fly in or the equipment they work with.

Be afraid. Be very afraid. Affirmative action does not merely lead to mass murder and civil war—that's just for starters. Before long, bridges will collapse and planes will plummet from the sky, and every time they do you'll know that some incompetent affirmative action hire is to blame.

Why, then, has the private sector gradually embraced affirmative action, with all these incompetent minorities eating away at our social infrastructure? Here's Sowell's stab at an explanation:

> Court decisions legitimizing affirmative action under prescribed conditions then provided businesses with a set of guidelines that could minimize their legal jeopardy. Therefore, when efforts were made to end group preferences and quotas during the 1980s by some within the [President Ronald] Reagan administration, big business support for the continuation of affirmative action helped doom the efforts to rescind it.

What in the world does "therefore" mean in this passage? Sure, minimal "legal jeopardy" is good, but wouldn't no legal jeopardy be better? Dodging this question, Sowell then writes, "In addition, large corporations tend to have their own internal affirmative action officials and departments, with their own vested interests in the continuation of such policies." Aha, those vested interests. The idea that large corporations might not want to be seen as racist or sexist employers, like the idea that large corporations really mean it when they say that affirmative action has given them a deeper pool of efficient employees, seems never to have crossed Sowell's mind.

It's hard to imagine how any researcher could wonder aloud why white guys who'd once competed . . . with about 44 percent of the population might resist policies that put them in competition with the other 60 percent.

Empirical Studies

What social scientists will find most puzzling—or galling—about Sowell's book, though, is his dogged insistence that affirmative action has never been tested empirically, that there are no studies of its effects, no cost/benefit analyses of its policies. Faye Crosby's latest work, *Affirmative Action Is Dead; Long Live Affirmative Action*, provides a compact, ready-to-hand rebuttal of claims like these, crammed as it is with studies, surveys, assessments and a battery of psychological and attitudinal tests. At the same time, Crosby's book might also stand as an index of the naïveté of some of the people devising those tests. She repeatedly professes bewilderment at opposition to affirmative action: "Why, I wonder, has affirmative action in employment and education not been universally and vigorously supported in the United States?"

The nation's demographics will render affirmative action increasingly troublesome in the next quarter-century.

Perhaps Crosby's profession of puzzlement is merely for rhetorical effect, but it's hard to imagine how any researcher could wonder aloud why white guys who'd once competed for college placements, jobs and promotions with about 44 percent of the population, might resist policies that put them in competition with the other 60 percent. And Crosby seems to think that many people oppose affirmative action largely because they're misinformed about it: "For some time I have had no doubt that much of the resistance to affirmative action is based on misconceptions about the policy.... The policy implications of this conclusion would seem to be clear. Just teach people how affirmative action really operates, and the controversy will die down." Really? Crosby herself seems unsure of this. Although she says that for many Republicans and libertarians, "opposition to policies that resemble affirmative action derives more from a dislike of government intervention than from racial prejudice," she also concedes that "for overt and covert racists and sexists, the knowledge that affirmative action benefits those who have been previously excluded or oppressed may be what bothers them about the policy." But I doubt any of this is news in 2005. At the close of her book, Crosby proposes experiments that test people's support for affirmative action relative to their ideas about justice, but it's a mystery to me why she didn't devise those experiments and conduct them herself.

It Depends on What It Means

Then again, thanks to Crosby, I've gotten the distinct sense that such tests are part of the problem: She cites—and has conducted—study after study in which people are asked whether they approve of Company X, which gives "slight preferences for qualified women and ethnic minorities," or Company Y, which gives "strong preferences to qualified women and ethnic minorities, even if we must turn away better qualified or more highly skilled non-minority applicants." And guess what? In study after study, people approve of Company X's policies but not Company Y's—without being told that, as a matter of fact, Company Y's policies are illegal in the United States. On the one hand, this result suggests that more people would support affirmative action if they knew what it does and does not entail; on the other hand, it suggests that these very tests may be muddying rather than clarifying the issue. Perhaps it is no wonder that so many Americans believe affirmative action involves precisely the kind of racial quotas and set-asides that have been struck down by courts time and again; to gauge by studies like these, professional psychologists and sociologists have managed to spread disinformation about affirmative action as effectively as a whole think tank full of Sowells.

As Anderson points out at the close of *The Pursuit of Fairness*, the nation's demographics will render affirmative action increasingly troublesome in the next quarter-century, not only because the sons and daughters of the new African-American professional class are now entering colleges and workplaces but also because integration and immigration have produced something like a melting pot or a glorious mosaic or a dead metaphor of hybrid hyphenated identities. This outcome has further complicated a system that, as Nathan Glazer (who recently recast himself as a supporter of affirmative action) has remarked, already grants affirmative action status to people from Argentina and Spain but not Brazil or Portugal, and considers everyone from the Middle East to be white.

But our confusions are not simply demographic. As Scott Jaschik reported [in the summer of 2004] in the *Boston Globe*, "The University of Michigan released enrollment figures for next fall showing that the number of black students in its freshman class would be declining by as much as 13 percent. That same day, Texas A&M University—a school that refuses to consider race or ethnicity in admissions—announced its own numbers for the fall. Enrollment would be going up—dramatically—for all minority groups, including a whopping 57 percent increase for black students." Apparently, Michigan's response to *Gratz v. Bollinger* produced a more complex application process that contributed to an overall 18 percent drop in applications; meanwhile, Texas A&M, an all-white school until 1963, announced ... that it would abolish "legacy" admissions and began recruiting low-income students from urban areas. Clearly, Texas A&M sent somebody the right signal about race and justice, while Michigan is left to explore the imponderables of unintended consequences. And if the history of affirmative action is any guide, all we will be able to predict about the experiment is that both its intended and unintended results will surprise us—and compel us to think again, and yet again, about how best to foster justice for all.

Affirmative Action Is Necessary and Is Not Special Treatment

Kimberle Crenshaw

Kimberle Crenshaw is a professor of law at the University of California, Los Angeles, and she is executive director of the African American Policy Forum, a think tank.

Ruthie Stevenson was on her way to the post office in Mt. Clemens, [Michigan], when she was asked to sign a petition to "make civil rights fairer for everybody." The circulator named the president of the local NAACP [National Association for the Advancement of Colored People] as a supporter. This would have been surprising, since the petition—known euphemistically as the Michigan Civil Rights Initiative—sought to amend the Michigan constitution to eliminate all affirmative-action programs in the state. Moreover, Stevenson knew firsthand that fraud was afoot: *She* was the president of the local NAACP, and had certainly never lent her support.

Fraud and Deception

Unfortunately, Stevenson was far from the only Michigan voter to have encountered trickery and deception in Ward Connerly's campaign to eliminate affirmative action. Hundreds of Michigan citizens, disproportionately African American, testified before the Michigan Civil Rights Commission and later in federal district court that Connerly's canvassers lied or otherwise misled them to secure their signatures.

The federal district court judge denounced what it called voter fraud, but ruled that the effort deceived blacks and whites equally, and thus did not violate the Voting Rights Act.

Kimberle Crenshaw, "A Preference for Deception," *Ms. Magazine*, vol. 18, no. 1, Winter 2008, pp. 39–41. Copyright © 2008 *Ms. Magazine*. Reproduced by permission.

The court noted, however, "If the proposal eventually passes, it will be stained by well-documented acts of fraud and deception that the defendants, as a matter of fact, have not credibly denied." The proposal did pass, in November of 2006. Michigan thus becomes the third state to ratify such an initiative, with all three long and divisive campaigns fronted by Connerly. Yet the stain predicted by the court is barely visible to those who haven't witnessed the seamy underbelly of his supposedly highbrow efforts.

The most audacious dimension of Connerly's masquerade, which he now hopes to replicate in five other states in November [2008], is his use of the language of civil rights as the Trojan horse to roll his reactionary agenda into the center of American politics. By selectively sampling from its martyr, Dr. Martin Luther King Jr., Connerly has appropriated the terminology, symbolism and moral authority of the civil rights movement to undo some of its most important victories. The millions of U.S. citizens who are primed to affirm any proposal framed as advancing civil rights are precisely those most at risk of being tricked into voting against their own interests. Women and black people were *denied* the vote in the past; today, they are *deceived* out of their votes.

Connerly's Civil Rights Initiative (CRI) campaigns use purposefully deceptive language to confuse some voters into repudiating policies they might otherwise support. Virtually all his campaigns purport to ban "discrimination and preference" on the basis of race, sex, color, ethnicity or national origin. Even those who read the language of his initiatives with caution will not necessarily recognize a ban on discrimination or preference as a vote to end affirmative action.

Preference and Discrimination

For many voters, "preference" does not equate with affirmative action. Instead, it captures the bevy of rewards afforded to those who have been historically advantaged in American society through nepotism, old-boy networks and discriminatory enclaves. These and other exclusionary practices function as built-in preferences that funnel a disproportionate share of resources and opportunities to whites and to men.

While Americans overwhelmingly oppose "racial preference," a clear majority support "affirmative action."

Voters who understand that dynamic may thus interpret *preference* as a way of describing *discrimination*—and thus a vote for a CRI is a vote against entrenched and systemic exclusion. Probably tens of thousands of voters in Michigan, and previously in Washington and California, voted for Connerly's initiatives in error. The obvious solution is for voters to be presented with clear language indicating that the real purpose of the initiatives is to eliminate affirmative-action programs for women and people of color.

But Connerly has repeatedly rejected this simple solution. Despite his claims that the majority of Americans stand with him, he has refused to use plain language, instead obscuring the real purpose of these initiatives. And it's obvious why: As early as 1992, the distinguished pollster Louis Harris discovered that while Americans overwhelmingly oppose "racial preference," a clear majority support "affirmative action." For some Americans, the words "racial preference" trigger images of rigid quotas, reverse discrimination and unqualified minorities, while "affirmative action" has come to mean increasing opportunities for members of excluded or underrepresented groups. Harris thus concluded that how the question is worded on this issue is highly significant.

Support for Affirmative Action

In fact, when the city of Houston changed the wording of a Connerly initiative in that city to pose a direct question to voters about whether affirmative-action policies should be banned, the initiative lost. But when elected officials and courts allowed him to use his deceptive language in California and Washington, the initiatives passed.

So Connerly has fought hard to ensure that his initiatives reach the ballot only with the deceptive language of "discrimination and preference." But at least in Missouri, one of the five states Connerly has targeted for a "Super Tuesday" CRI campaign, the tables have been turned. The secretary of state wrote a ballot summary that clarified the initiative's objective of eliminating affirmative action. Predictably, Connerly's team has filed suit, claiming that the term is "ambiguous, overinclusive and value-laden."

From police and fire departments to courtrooms and boardrooms, affirmative action has opened doors of opportunity.

While it is true that "affirmative action" is subject to competing interpretations, most voters understand that it refers to some form of race- or gender-targeted programs. And Connerly knows that the majority of Americans support a whole host of such programs—particularly those that offer development, mentoring and outreach for women, girls and people of color. Yet when the ban on "preferences" passes, emboldened critics wield the CRI as a weapon to bludgeon all affirmative-action programs. Thus, programs requiring contractors to verify outreach efforts to women- and minority-owned businesses, or race- or gender-targeted health screening programs, or even domestic-violence shelters, have all been subject to a CRI assault.

Women Benefit

Since women are a sizable, multiracial, multigenerational and cross-class bloc of voters, their collective political muscle could stop Connerly's initiatives in their tracks. Moreover, women are not simply potential allies in the struggle to maintain affirmative action; they are its principal beneficiaries. Affirmative action has helped integrate them into all sectors of the American economy. From police and fire departments to courtrooms and boardrooms, affirmative action has opened doors of opportunity for women to enter.

Yet the women's vote, as it turns out, is no silver bullet of a solution. While women of color oppose Connerly overwhelmingly, white women in all three state CRI elections have voted decisively for his initiatives. In Michigan, for example, an exit poll showed that 59 percent of white women voted for the CRI, while 82 percent of women of color voted against it. Not only are women *not* a coherent voting bloc on this issue, they're more divided on it than men are.

Perhaps one reason for this divide is that white women are virtually invisible targets of the CRI assault on affirmative action, as the CRI strategy has been to ignore them as beneficiaries of affirmative action in favor of targeting people of color, especially African Americans. This may well lead many white women to imagine themselves not as beneficiaries of these policies but as those *aggrieved* by them. Connerly's capacity to stir up fears about affirmative action is easily facilitated by a media that does virtually nothing to deepen understanding of this vital issue. According to a Fairness & Accuracy in Reporting study, not only does mainstream media consistently describe affirmative-action policies as preferential and discriminatory, it rarely mentions women as beneficiaries of the policies or discusses the exclusionary barriers affirmative action is designed to dismantle.

Affirmative Action Is Necessary

Since Alan Bakke's famous [reverse-discrimination] lawsuit against the University of California's Davis Medical School in 1978, most of the symbolic *victims* of affirmative action have been white women—such as Jennifer Gratz and Barbara Grutter, lead plaintiffs in the University of Michigan affirmative-action cases decided by the U.S. Supreme Court in 2003. They were not likely chosen to play this victim role by accident.

The effort to fully mobilize women to resist this assault on affirmative action will require us to tap the deepest traditions of antiracist feminism and remind all women of their own very real experiences with discrimination in disparate sectors of American society. A key step will be to reframe the terms of this debate so that affirmative-action policies are properly associated with the elimination of unwarranted *obstacles* faced by white women and people of color.

It is helpful, too, to recognize that the rallying cry of "special treatment" is not at all new: Virtually all efforts to integrate excluded groups into American institutions have been denounced in those terms. Similarly, efforts to integrate women into all-male institutions (such as private clubs) have been resisted as unnatural, unjustified and disruptive. But interestingly, as those male-dominated environments become suspect and eventually unacceptable, efforts to change the rules are no longer seen as special treatment but as perfectly reasonable policies to equalize opportunity.

The challenge for us in contemporary America is to capture this understanding across a range of modern institutions, where the presence of women and people of color remains a matter of controversy rather than a normal fact of life. As long as such situations remain, policies designed to ensure their presence are going to be criticized as special treatment and thus unfair. If efforts to defend affirmative action are going to be successful, advocates will have to redirect the public's attention to the conditions of everyday life for women and minorities that are themselves unfair, and to which affirmative action is a modest but a very necessary solution.

Affirmative Action Is a Necessary Part of the Solution to Racism

Ellis Cose

Ellis Cose is a columnist and a contributing editor for Newsweek. *He is the author of* Bone to Pick: Of Forgiveness, Reconciliation, Reparation, and Revenge.

Affirmative action has been under assault since it came into existence. But of late, the scent of blood has been in the air. There is a sense among certain of its foes that the policy is in its final throes, reeling like a battered boxer in the ring, merely awaiting the final blow. "The nation has lost its patience with it. There may be some ups and downs in the course of human events with regard to this, but it's ending. There's no question about it in my mind. *It's ending.* So what we need to be doing is saying, 'How do we make this transition from a paradigm in which race just seeps out of every pore of the body politic, where we think that the only way to solve social problems is race, to one that is more acceptable to more people and more directly addresses the problems of the people?'"

The Initiative Movement

So declared Ward Connerly, a self-made political operator and entrepreneur, and a uniquely American character: a black man who has declared war on the government programs that many women and people of color credit with giving them a toehold in the middle class.

Connerly's crowning achievement is the passage of a California ballot initiative called Proposition 209. This November [2006] will mark the 10-year anniversary of the vote on that measure, which ended state-run affirmative action programs. The proposition did not spawn—as some feared it would—a nation-wide citizens' revolt against so-called race and gender preferences. But it sent tremors through the civil rights community. In 1997, Connerly took the fight to Houston but failed to convince voters there to pass a ballot measure that would have ended affirmative action in city government. The next year, he succeeded in passing Initiative 200, which was Washington state's version of Proposition 209. After that, Connerly's initiative movement effectively collapsed. Connerly did gear up the machinery in Florida in 1999 but was outmaneuvered by [Governor] Jeb Bush, who issued an executive order banning most affirmative action programs, which made the ballot initiative moot. After that, foes of affirmative action focused more attention on the courts. But recently Connerly has come roaring back.

To believe in affirmative action . . . is to believe (say antagonists and some supporters as well) in a concept of equality turned upside down.

This November [2006], Michigan voters are being asked to give their blessing to another Connerly-sponsored initiative [the initiative passed]—one that arose largely out of discontent with a pair of Supreme Court decisions. Those decisions, handed down in June 2003, reviewed admissions policies for the University of Michigan's law school and its undergraduate College of Literature, Science, and the Arts. The high court upheld the university's right to use race in the pursuit of "diversity," even as it condemned the way the undergraduate school had chosen to do so. . . .

The Reason for the Debate

All of which raises a question: Why are we still wrestling with this stuff? Why, more than a quarter of a century after the high court ruled race had a legitimate place in university admissions decisions, are we still fighting over whether race should play a role in who gets in and who does not? Why, given the well-documented history of discrimination in America against women and various ethnic and racial groups, are we still debating whether programs that attempt to address that history belong in the public sphere? One answer is that principled people on both sides of the issue have fundamentally different views of the world and different takes on the future. Another is that the very idea of affirmative action—defined, in this sense, as systematically treating members of various groups differently in the pursuit of diversity or social justice—strikes some people as downright immoral. The debate is not about whether society should offer equal opportunity. Even opponents of affirmative action programs claim they support *that*. The battle is over what, and who, should be sacrificed in its name. To believe in affirmative action, as defined above, is to believe (say antagonists and some supporters as well) in a concept of equality turned upside down. It is to believe that "to treat some persons equally, we must treat them differently," as famously put by U.S. Supreme Court Justice Harry Blackmun in 1978. It is to believe, in other words, something many Americans refuse to believe: that our country falls so far short of delivering on its promise of equality that members of designated disadvantaged groups must be given special consideration. . . .

California's Proposition 209

Prior to its passage, proponents of [California's Prop 209] were fond of arguing that minority students would benefit because they would finally be free of the "stigma" associated with affirmative action. They would be accepted as equal to their white peers, went the argument, since they had met the same standards. California's experience seems to say that assumption is not necessarily true—at least not yet. The stigma seems to linger, as any number of students told me and as Evan Caminker discovered. "While I was associate dean [at Michigan] in 2002, maybe it was early 2003," he said, "I was part of the legal team representing the law school in the *Grutter* case. My former students at UCLA—who wanted to write an amicus brief in the case—and I had many converstions . . . about what they wanted to say. And one of the most important, and I thought really poignant, messages that [the students communicated] was . . . to the extent that they felt there was still a stigma associated with being black or being Hispanic . . . that feeling [had not gone away]."

Much of the debate . . . is driven more by emotion and preconceptions than by any reasoned consideration of the facts.

Proposition 209 hasn't done anything for the cause of K through 12 education either, though it was sold, in part, as a way to get people focused on that problem. Everyone agrees that society would be significantly better off if more "disadvantaged minorities" naturally made it into the elite schools' pipeline. But ending affirmative action in California doesn't seem to have mobilized people to do anything about the pipeline problem. As former UC [University of California] President Richard Atkinson recently pointed out, nearly half of blacks and Latinos in California fail to finish high school: "By the time these minority students reach college-age, it is already too late for many of them; crime-ridden neighborhoods, poverty and failing K through 12 public schools are a brutal winnowing process." Yet as UCLA graduate student Kimberly Griffin pointed out, no movement has sprung up to address that range of issues.

Nor has Proposition 209 ushered in a better racial climate. Instead, according to several students I interviewed, it seems to have made honest racial dialogue a bit more difficult than it was.

It is also far from clear, as proponents of Proposition 209 insisted would be the case, that barring consideration of race results in a better match between university and student. Or that it improves graduation rates, since students who got into school on the basis of "merit," as opposed to affirmative action, supposedly would be more likely to succeed. On that question the evidence, at best, seems mixed. Since Proposition 209 passed, the six-year graduation rate of black and Hispanic students at UC Berkeley has gone up. But, as UC Berkeley officials are quick to point out, graduation rates were going up even before the proposition passed—and have continued to rise since. Indeed, they suspect the rates might have gone up even more had the measure failed. For Proposition 209 had the somewhat unexpected effect of disproportionately reducing the share of those black students whose families had some experience with college—and who presumably would have been more aware of what matriculating at a university required. Moreover, as Berkeley's chancellor pointed out, though black and Chicano students at Berkeley did not matriculate as quickly as whites or Asians, they "graduate at rates that are much higher than white students [at other public universities]." Meanwhile, at the University of Michigan, Ann Arbor, which continued to consider race in admissions, graduation rates for minority students also went up, which officials there attributed, in some measure, to their determination to ensure "the success of each and every one of them."

Old Assumptions

Despite the California experience, none of the proponents of Proposition 209 seem much interested in revising their old assumptions. That is not particularly surprising. Nor is it surprising that much of the debate over Proposition 209, like many discussions about race, is driven more by emotion and preconceptions than by any reasoned consideration of the facts. But that does get in the way of seeing what is actually going on or of opening minds to the possibility that some cherished, though unexamined, assumptions might conceivably be wrong.

It is widely assumed, for instance, that picking students with the most stellar academic records will result in a better class—and that all of the students selected will be the better for it. But Scott Page, professor of political science and economics at the University of Michigan, thinks that may not be true. It does not necessarily follow, he argues, that "if we get smarter students individually they're going to collectively be smarter." Instead, students might profit more (intellectually and otherwise) from interacting with an assortment of students who have various intellectual gifts and widely ranging experience, as opposed to interacting merely with those who perform well on a narrow range of academic measures.

Too often in the dialogue about affirmative action, important questions remain unasked and assumptions reign.

In his forthcoming book, *A Logic of Diversity*, Page writes about a computer simulation he ran while a professor at Cal Tech that examined how various groups confronted a difficult problem: "In working through the implications of my model, I stumbled upon a counterintuitive finding: diverse groups of problem solvers—groups of people with diverse tools—consistently outperformed groups of the best and the brightest: if I formed two groups: one random (and therefore diverse) and one consisting of the best individual performers, the first group almost always did better. In my model, *diversity trumped ability.*"

The Goal of Universities

My intention here is neither to prove nor refute Page's thesis, but instead to make the point that the matter of who should get into any group (or institution) cannot be separated from the question of what that group (or institution) hopes to accomplish. Is it the job of public universities to select only those who have already proven they can do stellar academic work and to write off the rest? Or is their job to educate a leadership cadre for an ever-more diverse society? Should universities select those individuals who, collectively, will perform best, even if that means rejecting many people who, individually, perform better? Or should they do something altogether different? The answer one gets, of course, depends on the question asked. And too often in the dialogue about affirmative action, important questions remain unasked and assumptions reign.

In his memoir, Connerly tells the story of meeting with a couple—the husband was a physicist and the wife an academic accountant—who were upset that their son had been rejected by all five UC medical schools, despite his outstanding academic accomplishments. Connerly found the school's decisions inexplicable and outrageous, especially given that the son had been accepted by a number of other prestigious schools, including a joint program of Harvard and MIT [Massachusetts Institute of Technology]. To Connerly, the parents' story was evidence of "rigged" admissions, a system that was corrupt to its very core—and potent ammunition in his fight against preferences. But one could also read the story quite differently, as evidence of a university system that had a much broader mission than merely rewarding those who had already had every educational advantage and therefore stood at the head of the class.

There is little doubt society would be better off if affirmative action did not exist, provided that the problems that gave it life did not exist as well; just as there is little doubt society would be better off without prisons, provided there were no lawbreakers to put in them. But no one—not even those most concerned about unfairness in the justice system—are arguing that we should do away with jails.

Time alone will not solve the problems that gave affirmative action life.

[According to the Court's opinion in *Grutter v. Bollinger* in 2003,] "The Court expects that 25 years from now, the use of racial preferences will no longer be necessary to further the interest approved today." I have yet to speak to any deep thinker who takes Sandra Day O'Connor's rather offhand comment seriously. Those opposed to affirmative action see the comment as nothing more than a delaying tactic, an attempt to extend indefinitely into the future a policy they see as indefensible. Those who favor affirmative action view it as "aspirational, an expression of hope," in the words of Reginald Turner, past president of the National Bar Association. "I share her hope that our society will be more egalitarian 25 years from now than it is today," said Turner.

[Affirmative action] began as a modest attempt to give a bit of a boost to a handful of folks from a race of people who had been unfairly held back for centuries.

O'Connor's comment notwithstanding, time alone will not solve the problems that gave affirmative action life. Progress does not happen on its own accord. In his "Letter from Birmingham City Jail," Martin Luther King weighed in on what he called the "tragic misconception" about time. "It is the strangely irrational notion that there is something in the very flow of time that will inevitably cure all ills. Actually time is neutral. It can be used either destructively or constructively. . . . We must come to see that human progress never rolls in on wheels of inevitability. It comes through the tireless efforts and persistent work of men willing to be co-workers with God, and without this hard work time itself becomes an ally of the forces of social stagnation."

The Role of Affirmative Action

Just as time alone will not solve America's race-related problems, neither will affirmative action. The fundamental problem with (and the dilemma of) affirmative action is that it was never meant to carry the weight society has thrown on its shoulders. It was never meant to rescue the poor. It was never supposed to enlighten the illiterate, make the sick well, or feed the hungry. It was not meant to make up for the inadequacies of a bad K through 12 education; or, for that matter, to make up for the deficiencies that develop well before children even get to kindergarten. It began as a modest attempt to give a bit of a boost to a handful of folks from a race of people who had been unfairly held back for centuries. But because we, as a nation, lacked the will or knowledge to solve the big problems, we charged affirmative action with doing it all. And it morphed into something both grand (in terms of public perception) and small (in terms of its actual impact), making it vulnerable not only to criticism of its not being effective, but also of its being too onerous and of violating the very spirit of the equal treatment it is supposed to remedy or promote.

The choice society faces is not about ending affirmative action—at some point, as both its critics and defenders agree, the affirmative action tugboat will run out of steam. The question is whether, before that happens, society will find the will and resources to vanquish the problems that gave rise to it in the first place. No child chooses to be born into poverty with parents who are semi-literate or to live in neighborhoods where the schools are little more than holding pens, where dropping out is more common than graduating. No child chooses to be told, virtually from the moment of consciousness, that achievement is not an option.

In an essay exploring the so-called skills gap between blacks and whites, University of Chicago economist Derek Neal highlighted a small study begun in the early 1970s. That study convincingly demonstrated that high-quality preschool programs could go a long way toward permanently closing the performance gap. "The first generation of black children to enter kindergarten with the same basic language and arithmetic skills as white children may well be the first generation of black adults to enter the labor market on equal footing with their white peers," he concluded. The cause of early childhood education would seem a natural for the proponents of anti-affirmative action initiatives. Yet, for the most part, they seem uninterested in that fight which, if successful, really could render affirmative action irrelevant within O'Conner's 25-year deadline.

Richard Atkinson, former president of the UC system, saw two big lessons in California's experience with Proposition 209: "The first is that race-neutral admissions policies drastically and demonstrably limit the ability of elite universities to reflect the diversity of a multicultural state in any meaningful way. The second is that we will never resolve the conflict over affirmative action by an appeal to the values invoked on both sides of the issue. The dynamics of the public debate create a situation in which compromise is impossible because each side claims the moral high ground."

Both sides do indeed claim the moral high ground, making compromise on issues associated with affirmative action difficult. In a sane world, the battle in Michigan, and indeed the battle over affirmative action writ large, would offer an opportunity to seriously engage a question the enemies and defenders of affirmative action claim to care about: How do you go about creating a society where all people—not just the lucky few—have the opportunities they deserve? It is a question much broader than the debate over affirmative action. But until we begin to move toward an answer, the debate over affirmative action will continue—even if it is something of a sideshow to what should be the main event.

Affirmative Action Promotes Diversity

Mark A. Emmert

Mark A. Emmert is the president of the University of Washington.

Access to equal opportunity distinguishes and strengthens the United States. The country has aggressively pursued this ideal over the past 50 years with federal policies and court decisions that opened colleges and universities to ethnic and racial populations that had historically been vastly underrepresented.

Affirmative action, the federal program that was most influential in helping build diverse campuses, has been slowly but demonstrably eroded over the past 10 years through a combination of statewide referenda and now the latest Supreme Court decision limiting the use of race in school choice.

These incursions have occurred despite the conviction of a vast array of business leaders, government officials, and university administrators that for the past 35 years, affirmative action has been a remarkably successful tool in the quest for equity in access to higher education.

Five key states—collectively enrolling over half a million students each year—currently are operating under severe constraints regarding the use of race as a factor in admissions decisions. The electorate in three states—California, Washington, and Michigan—has emphatically voted to abolish the use of affirmative action in public university admissions. Two other populous states—Texas and Florida—have implemented admissions processes that have limited or eliminated the use of

Mark A. Emmert, "Confronting a New Era of Diversity," *The Christian Science Monitor*, August 6, 2007, p. 9. Copyright © 2007 Christian Science Monitor. Reproduced by permission of the author.

affirmative action. On the horizon, we can see efforts to eradicate affirmative action being mounted in additional states for the 2008 election cycle.

Affirmative action has been a remarkably successful tool in the quest for equity in access to higher education.

What had been a national policy is being dismantled, state by state. Each state that has abandoned affirmative action has had to ascertain separately its legal ability and the boundaries that would allow it to foster diversity. Because each state's context differs, America is developing fragmented solutions to the challenge of maintaining a diverse student body, a challenge that many courts continue to see as a "compelling interest" for the nation.

Fostering Diversity

And because the US has gone from a national policy to a set of disparate solutions, it faces a conundrum: Even as university leaders in post-affirmative-action states support the goals of a highly diversified student body, they must show that without the tool of affirmative action, they can still build a diverse, talented, highly competitive student population.

For university presidents and administrators like myself, who have grown up in a world where affirmative action was solidly embraced, it has been an awakening to find ourselves leading institutions that must now accomplish diversity without using the tool of affirmative action. I recognize the significant role that policy has played, and I do not wish its elimination where it is still permitted. But without it, we must work very hard to increase all types of diversity at our institutions.

In the states that have had to create new policies in the absence of affirmative action, there have been successes and disappointments, and we have seen that it can take years to begin to recover from the elimination of this tool.

Alternatives to Affirmative Action

What we discovered in Washington was that there are other ways to ensure diversity and access to higher education, particularly by taking socioeconomic factors into account. One essential element was undertaking an intensive effort to encourage more students from disadvantaged backgrounds to apply to the university. This meant convincing them that there was indeed a place for them at an institution like ours, that they were welcome, and that they could be successful here.

Additionally, we had to find a way to take economic considerations off the table. Many universities, including Washington, have instituted programs ensuring that students from low and lower-middle income families will be able to attend college tuition-free, creating a compelling new approach to diversity and recognizing the impact of economic standing.

We have also adopted a holistic admissions review process, a labor-intensive enterprise that is well worth the effort. The more we can know about each individual student who applies, the better informed our admissions decisions are. The results so far are promising: The academic level of our entering students is as good as it had been prior to holistic review, and the student body is more diverse.

All of us—whether or not we still can use affirmative action—need to pool our collective experience and data to establish the best ways of being accessible to applicants from all strata of our society. We know that critical elements include increased outreach, improvements to financial aid, and holistic admission models. We have been told by corporate leaders, by elected officials, and by the armed forces, that more diverse organizations are better organizations. Indeed, our own experiences in overseeing universities demonstrates this fact. Entry to our universities and colleges provides the opportunity for many to rise economically and improve their lives and add to the vigor of our nation. It is a key to our future success and should be accessible to all.

Affirmative Action Harms Minority Students

Terry Eastland

Terry Eastland is publisher of The Weekly Standard *and the author of* Ending Affirmative Action.

Affirmative action emerged in the 1960s as a policy intended to help blacks. How, then, would institutions committed to affirmative action respond if it could be shown that the policy does blacks more harm than good? Richard Sander, a law professor at UCLA, is about to find out.

A Study Reveals Surprising Results

This week [January 3, 2005,] the *Stanford Law Review* will publish his article, "A Systemic Analysis of Affirmative Action in American Law Schools." By "affirmative action" in the law schools, Sander means the racially preferential variety used in admissions, and his focus is exclusively on preferences extended to blacks, the original beneficiary group, the other such groups having been added later (and for less compelling reasons).

The title of the 117-page study is as dull as Sander's conclusion is sharp. "What I find and describe," he writes, "is a system of racial preferences that, in one realm after another, produces more harms than benefits for its putative beneficiaries." Sander makes the further, riveting point that "the annual production of new black lawyers would probably increase if racial preference were abolished tomorrow."

Who is Richard Sander anyway? Perhaps not the man you would imagine from the analysis above. A lifelong Democrat, a liberal on most issues, he has a long record of involvement in civil rights issues, including housing segregation. His son is biracial. "So the question," he notes in the article, "of how non-whites are treated and how they fare in higher education gives rise in me to all the doubts and worries of a parent." Because he favors race-conscious strategies in principle, his article is a classic instance of following an argument wherever it leads. At *volokh.com*—the blog where he summarized his findings—he wrote that he was "surprised and dismayed" by his "generally negative conclusions," which "put me at odds with many close friends."

In an interview, he told me there could be "a significant professional cost" for having written the article, which is already under attack. But he remains confident of his findings, and he's prepared to defend them. He'll reply to critics in a future issue of the law review. And he's writing a book looking at the impact of affirmative action on all favored groups, not just blacks.

The Data

There's something else to report about Sander, perhaps the most important thing. Besides being a lawyer, he's also an economist. And "A Systemic Analysis" is plainly the work of an economist. Sander doesn't address the familiar legal issues involved with affirmative action (no parsing or strict scrutiny here) but instead asks whether preferences "meet their simplest goals of producing more and better black lawyers."

To answer it, Sander needed relevant data. Through FOIA [Freedom of Information Act] requests he collected 2002 and 2003 admissions data from seven public law schools, some of them among the nation's very best. He also worked from the data gathered by the Law School Admission Council [LSAC] on one national cohort of law students—27,000 students who entered law school in 1991. LSAC, which tracked the students (representing 95 percent of all accredited law schools) through

1997, collected information on the students' admissions credentials (LSAT score and undergraduate GPA), race, academic performance, and bar exam outcomes.

The cascading effect leaves most black students "mismatched" with peers whose academic credentials . . . are superior.

Sander was working with his data sets 18 months ago when the Supreme Court upheld the admissions preferences used by the Michigan law school. Justice O'Connor's opinion for the Court in *Grutter v. Bollinger* [2003] accepted the notion advanced by Michigan and its large roster of amici that preferences benefit those they target, which in this case included blacks, Latinos, and Native Americans. Sander had come to the opposite conclusion, and what he noticed about the Michigan law school case (and its companion case from the University of Michigan) was, he told me, how "saturated" they were with social science. "So much of it was really bad. That was one of the reasons I wrote [the article]."

Preferences and Mismatch Effects

In the picture Sander draws, the admissions preferences for blacks are very large. This is the case with respect to almost all law schools. Which is to say, contrary to conventional wisdom, preferences aren't confined to the elite schools. Indeed, "affirmative action has a cascading effect through American legal education." The top-tier law schools enroll not only the small number of blacks who don't need preferences to get in but also less-qualified black applicants whose credentials would have sufficed to gain them admission under a race-blind standard to a second-tier school. Second-tier schools are then forced to choose between having few if any black students (under a race-blind standard) or using preferences to reach *their* racial goals. The second-tier schools make the latter choice, and so the effects cascade to the third-tier schools and on down the law-school ladder. There is thus a "system" in place whose net effect is "to move nearly all blacks up a tier (or two) in the law school hierarchy." Only at the bottom—in the lowest-tier schools—do you find black students who are probably unqualified for any law school.

The cascading effect leaves most black students "mis-matched" with peers whose academic credentials (in terms of LSAT scores and UGPA) are superior. Which means, as Sander puts it, that "nearly all blacks [are placed] at an enormous academic disadvantage in the schools they attend." And so there are "mismatch effects." In their first year, about 50 per-cent of black law students end up in the bottom tenth of their class, and roughly two-thirds in the bottom fifth, with only 8 percent placing in the top half. The grades of black law school students go down a bit from the first to the third year. Black students have a much higher attrition rate than white students (19 percent compared with 8 percent). Sander finds that fact unsurprising, since students (of whatever race) with the very worst grades are those who are expelled or drop out. Finally, black law school graduates fail the bar exam at four times the rate of white graduates. Sander concludes that more than 40 percent of black students starting out to become lawyers never reach that goal.

Without mismatching and its effects, black students would perform better, fewer would fail to graduate, and 8 percent more would pass the bar.

Sander faults the preferences used to admit blacks for the systematic mismatch and its effects. He contends that black students perform the same academically as whites with similar test scores, and that if blacks were not mismatched, they would have better grades and learn more. And he adduces evi-dence showing that grades are powerful predictors of bar exam performance. Not incidentally, employers, he also found, prefer to hire graduates with good grades.

Eliminate Preferences

Sander envisions a law school universe without preferences, which is not, he says, "an unthinkable armageddon." There would be many fewer blacks enrolled in the top 20 schools, he says, but overall the number of black students would shrink only slightly—by about 14 percent. And without mismatching and its effects, black students would perform better, fewer would fail to graduate, and 8 percent more would pass the bar.

Because elite schools would have few black students—perhaps 1 or 2 percent of their student bodies—and because those schools fancy themselves as critical in shaping the views of future national leaders, Sander suggests "an intermediate step" by which the elite schools would still use preferences, but on a limited basis, such that a class is 4 percent (and not the current 7 to 8 percent) black. Sander says this would dampen the cascading and bring an end to mismatching "at some point fairly high in the law school spectrum." It would appear that Sander offers the 4 percent solution as a concession to elite opinion, a way to advance a dialogue on the costs and benefits of preferences, not because he believes in it himself. After all, his basic conclusion is this: "Blacks are the victims of law school programs of affirmative action, not the beneficiaries."

Response to the Study

To judge by the academic response so far, Sander is going to be busy discussing his analysis. A group including the main architect of the Michigan law school admissions policy has written an article disagreeing with Sander's conclusions, including his assessment of what would happen under race-blind admissions. They claim the black law school population would shrink by 35 to 45 percent, and that the number of black graduates who pass the bar would decline by 25 to 30 percent. But other academics working from Sander's data sets are reaching the same conclusion as he. If Sander wins the social-science battle, that could have repercussions in litigation over admissions preferences, especially in the Supreme Court, where one of the justices who voted to sustain the Michigan policy, Justice Stephen Breyer, practices a jurisprudence (applauded by liberals) that looks to the consequences of a policy in assessing its legal merit.

Sander's article promises to reopen an issue that seemed settled in *Grutter*, notwithstanding that it was a 5-to-4 decision. Sander even imagines the next major legal challenge to admissions preferences: a lawsuit brought by black plaintiffs "who were admitted, spent years and thousands of dollars on their educations, and then never passed the bar and never became lawyers—all because of the misleading double standards used by law schools to admit them, and the schools' failure to disclose to them the uniquely long odds against their becoming lawyers."

That would certainly disturb the sleep of all the law school admissions officers who breathed a sigh of satisfaction after *Grutter*.

Affirmative Action Harms Minority Professionals

Stuart Taylor Jr.

Stuart Taylor Jr. is a nonresident senior fellow of governance studies at the Brookings Institution, a Newsweek *contributing editor, and a columnist for the* National Journal.

Most—if not all—of the nation's leading law firms seek to become more diverse by using "very large hiring preferences" for African-Americans and smaller preferences for Hispanics. So most of their newly hired minority lawyers have relatively weak academic records that would have brought rejection had they been white.

Racial Preferences at Law Firms

But these preferences are at best a mixed blessing—and are often a curse—for their recipients. After a year or two on the job, most minority associates at big firms get less desirable assignments and less training than their white counterparts. Many become discouraged and embittered. Young black lawyers leave big firms "at two or three times the rate of whites."

These problems plague minority lawyers precisely because of the racial preferences that got most of them hired. By lowering the big firms' usual hiring standards, large preferences bring "disparities in expectations and performance that ultimately hurt the intended beneficiaries."

These are among the conclusions copiously documented by Richard Sander, a UCLA law professor, in a 66-page article published in the *North Carolina Law Review*. It is laden with meticulous statistical analyses of six publicly available data sets, including surveys of thousands of law students and law-yers at various stages in their lives and careers.

Sander's blockbuster article, "The Racial Paradox of the Corporate Law Firm," rejects the conventional wisdom that racism explains why most young black lawyers in large firms do not fare well, and why barely 1 percent of big-firm part-ners—compared with 8 percent of new hires—are black.

After a year or two on the job, most minority associates at big firms get less desirable assignments and less train-ing than their white counterparts.

The paradox, Sander says, is that "aggressive racial prefer-ences at the law-school and law-firm level tend to undermine in some ways the careers of young attorneys and . . . contrib-ute to . . . the failure of the underlying goal of this whole pro-cess—the integration of elite firms at the partnership level."

Sander's analysis is a natural sequel to his stunning 115-page *Stanford Law Review* article in 2004 showing how the enormous racial preferences used by all selective law schools backfire against black students.

By producing huge black-white gaps in entering academic credentials, these preferences ensure that black students are clustered near the bottom of their classes, with only 8 percent ranking in the top half. This in turn explains why more than 43 percent of entering black law students never become law-yers.

Many a professor has attacked Sander's controversial 2004 analysis, but none has convincingly refuted it. And although the *North Carolina Law Review* twins Sander's latest article with a skillfully argued, 17-page, pro-preference rebuttal by Duke law professors James Coleman and Mitu Galati, its ulti-mate unpersuasiveness reinforces my confidence in Sander's analysis.

The Importance of Qualifications

Common sense tells those of us whose eyes are open that the pattern documented by Sander in the limited contexts of law schools and large firms also exists in college and other walks of life (although the scholarly Sander makes no such claim). Many capable African-Americans experience frustration and failure because racial preferences thrust them into elite settings where they compete against whites with far better qualifications. The root of the problem, of course, is that stunningly small percentages of blacks emerge from high school with strong academic skills.

Even though blacks make up only 1 or 2 percent of law students with high grades, they make up 8 percent of large law firm hires.

Preferential hiring of minorities with low grades. Large law firms feel enormous pressure—from corporate clients, the media, and others—to become more diverse. So for decades they have aggressively recruited black and Hispanic law students. Since very few have grades that meet the firms' usual standards, the firms hire many minorities with grades "far below those of the white students hired at the same firms."

Even though blacks make up only 1 or 2 percent of law students with high grades, they make up 8 percent of large law firm hires. One survey shows that at least 46 percent of black lawyers at large firms (compared with 14 percent of whites) had law school GPAs below 3.25. Fifty-six percent of these black lawyers admitted thinking that their race or ethnicity had been relatively important in winning them job offers.

How grades predict law firm success. It is "quite likely that the grade gap between whites and blacks in law school is duplicated in performance once inside the firm," Sander asserts.

In this, he challenges the popular myth that—in law and other vocations—grades do not predict future job performance.

Sander shows that large law firms pay very high salaries to attract the people with the highest law school grades. And available data bear out the firms' belief that these grades measure important skills.

To be sure, many outstanding lawyers did not have high grades. And many failures did. And skills such as jury appeal have little to do with grades. But very few big-firm lawyers appear before juries. And on average, Sander shows, law school grades measure "skills or qualities that continue to be relevant to effective performance throughout a legal career."

Surveys of University of Michigan Law School alumni, for example, find that those "with higher GPAs are more likely to survive the large-firm competition for partnerships" and earn more money.

The Perception of Racism

Racial disparities in training and assignments. Numerous surveys of young black lawyers in large firms show that "within a couple of years of starting associate jobs, many blacks and Hispanics have been largely relegated to routine, unchallenging work and deprived of most benefits of training, mentorship, and partner contact," Sander reports. Most minority lawyers do more "grunt work" than whites; have less contact with partners; report "frustration and a sense of failure"; and leave within the first few years.

Why? Surveys belie the views of some analysts that minority law students are less interested in corporate law firms than whites, Sander reports. Rather, the most plausible explanation is that although firms make collective decisions to use hiring preferences, the individual partners who dole out plum assignments have "an overwhelming incentive" to choose those perceived to be most able and "to shun those whom the attorney thinks for any reason may not be up to the job."

It's not about racism. Surveys show that a significant minority of young black and Hispanic lawyers in large firms perceive themselves to be victims of old-fashioned racial hostility on the job, Sander explains. But does this reflect reality? It's worth noting that 20 percent of entering black law students in one large survey thought they had been victims of discrimination in the admissions process—and that this was quite obviously the opposite of the truth.

Why would the same firms that use aggressive racial preferences to bring in minorities then turn around and discriminate against them? And why, if the firms are racist, are there virtually no complaints of discrimination in pay, hours of work, or overt treatment?

It's also telling that young blacks at firms with fewer than 50 lawyers—firms that do not use large racial preferences, the data show—report far, far fewer problems. There is no reason to suppose that these firms are more enlightened. The most plausible explanation, Sander shows, is that they hire minority lawyers who are well qualified for their jobs and whose work shows it.

Unless our large law firms, law schools, and other elite institutions moderate their racial double standards, they will continue to hurt many of the people they claim to be helping.

To be sure, some big-firm partners may well be twisted by racial animus, Sander says. But probably not very many. And it would not be hard for minority associates to find out who those partners are and avoid them.

On the other hand, Sander admits, it is "extraordinarily difficult" to sort out how much of the unhappy experience of black associates at large firms is due to individual skill deficiencies and how much is due to what scholars call "stereotype discrimination."

Some *individual* black associates "are entirely able to perform as well or better than white associates," Sander says. But even these associates may get inferior training and assignments if—as seems likely—the "merit gap [is] reinforced and unfairly extended through stereotyping generalizations" about racial groups. (Sander himself, by the way, has a half-black son and is no conservative.)

Such racial stereotyping is deplorable. But the main reason for its persistence is not white racism. It is the conspicuous use of large racial preferences. They advertise the assumption that minority lawyers (and others) cannot compete on their own merits, and they thrust them into high-level competitions that most are doomed to lose.

This tragedy will continue until we do a far better job of educating minority children. In the meantime, unless our large law firms, law schools, and other elite institutions moderate their racial double standards, they will continue to hurt many of the people they claim to be helping.

Affirmative Action Supports a View of African Americans as Victims

Dana White

Dana White served as international communications associate and director of the Washington Roundtable for the Asia-Pacific Press (WRAPP) at the Heritage Foundation.

When my grandfather grew up, white people told him he wasn't good enough, but black people said he was. When my father grew up, white people told him he couldn't compete, but black people said he could. So imagine my confusion when I saw blacks celebrating the Supreme Court's 5-4 decision affirming that blacks are indeed not good enough to get into the University of Michigan Law School.

It's ironic. Forty years after the Civil Rights Act was proposed in Congress, liberals insist blacks are incapable of meeting the same standards as whites. It's conservatives who believe in the limitless potential of blacks.

Thirty years ago, affirmative action may have been a necessary step to open the doors of American universities and companies. It helped to correct a history of racial discrimination propagated by whites, but it's a new day in America.

Today, blacks are the CEOs [chief executive officers] of American Express, AOL/Time Warner and Merrill Lynch. Oprah Winfrey is a billionaire and Colin Powell [and Condoleeza Rice have been] Secretary of State. This is not my grandfather's America.

Too many blacks do remain oppressed, but not by white Americans. Rather, it is by blacks who relish a perverse sub-culture of low standards and perpetual victimization. No longer do white racists tell black children books are for white people. Today, black people do this. Every day, black children suffer ridicule and disgrace for doing their homework, behaving in class, striving for excellence—in short, "acting white."

And within the perimeters of this black sub-culture, success is exalted only when it is earned in sports, music, dance, and in the Democratic Party. Should a black person succeed in other arenas, for example becoming secretary of state, Supreme Court justice or national security advisor, he or she is exiled from the race, his or her racial identity revoked.

Blacks as Victims

Within this sub-culture, blacks have narrowly defined the path to success and equate "black" with "victim." Condoleezza Rice? Not a victim, ergo not black. President Bill Clinton played the victim and was declared "the first black president."

Liberal black elites should stop preaching the rhetoric of perpetual oppression and encouraging all black people to be victims.

Other communities suffer systematic discrimination: Koreans, Chinese, Latinos and Jews, to name a few. But within these communities people encourage each other to go to school, get good grades and go to college. In some communities not earning a graduate degree is shameful. Only within the black community is academic or entrepreneurial success openly chastised.

Liberal black elites should stop preaching the rhetoric of perpetual oppression and encouraging all black people to be victims. Black leaders have done in 40 years what white people could not do in 400; they've made us accept inferior status.

It is time they told the truth about which blacks affirmative action helps. Affirmative action helps the children and the grandchildren of Jesse Jackson, John Conyers and Al Sharpton who have the money for the SAT prep courses, private schools and the clout to call the deans of admission should something go awry. Moreover, they all have the alumni status to get their children into their colleges and universities. Ironically, they all are able to do for their children what they complain that many white Americans have done routinely and systemically for generations.

It is time for liberal black leaders to stop hiding behind racism and admit that our priorities as a community have become our greatest hurdle to achieving long-term success. They must stop dismissing successful blacks, regardless of party affiliation, as exceptions in an otherwise victim-rich race. They must stop blaming white Americans for the sins of the past and set goals for the future. Most white Americans live in the 21st century; it is time more black Americans joined them.

Trying to Achieve Diversity Through Affirmative Action Is Racist

Jonah Goldberg

Jonah Goldberg is a contributing editor for National Review, *the founding editor of* National Review Online, *and a syndicated columnist.*

It's time to admit that "diversity" is code for racism. If it makes you feel better, we can call it "nice" racism or "well-intentioned" racism or "racism that's good for you." Except that's the rub: It's racism that may be good for you if "you" are a diversity guru, a rich white liberal, a college administrator or one of sundry other types. But the question of whether diversity is good for "them" is a different question altogether, and much more difficult to answer.

Minority Quotas

If by "them" you mean minorities such as Jews, Chinese Americans, Indian Americans and other people of Asian descent, then the ongoing national obsession with diversity probably isn't good. Indeed, that's why Jian Li, a freshman at Yale, filed a civil-rights complaint against Princeton University for rejecting him. Li had nigh-upon perfect test scores and grades, yet Princeton turned him down. He'll probably get nowhere with his complaint—he did get into Yale after all—but it shines a light on an uncomfortable reality.

"Theoretically, affirmative action is supposed to take spots away from white applicants and redistribute them to under-represented minorities," Li told the *Daily Princetonian*. "What's

Jonah Goldberg, "Racism by Any Other Name," *National Review Online*, November 15, 2006, p. L7. www.nationalreview.com. Copyright © 2006 by Tribune Media Services, Inc. Reproduced by permission.

happening is one segment of the minority population is losing places to another segment of minorities, namely Asians to underrepresented minorities."

Li points to a study conducted by two Princeton academics [in 2005] which concluded that if you got rid of racial preferences in higher education, the number of whites admitted to schools would remain fairly constant. However, without racial preferences, Asians would take roughly 80 percent of the positions now allotted to Hispanic and black students.

In other words, there is a quota—though none dare call it that—keeping Asians out of elite schools in numbers disproportionate to their merit. This is the same sort of quota once used to keep Jews out of the Ivy League—not because of their lack of qualifications, but because having too many Jews would change the "feel" of, say, Harvard or Yale. Today, it's the same thing, only we've given that feeling a name: diversity.

No Benefits to Diversity

The greater irony is that it is far from clear that diversity is good for black students either. Peter Kirsanow, a member of the U.S. Commission on Civil Rights, notes that there is now ample empirical data showing that the supposed benefits of diversity in education are fleeting when real and often are simply nonexistent. Black students admitted to universities above their skill level often do poorly and fail to graduate in high numbers. UCLA law professor Richard Sander found that nearly half of black law students reside in the bottom ten percent of their law-school classes. If they went to schools one notch down, they might do far better.

Kirsanow asks: "Would college administrators continue to mouth platitudes about affirmative action if their students knew that preferential admissions cause black law students to flunk out at two-and-a-half times the rate of whites? Or that black law students are six times less likely to pass the bar? Or that half of black law students never become lawyers?"

Making Preferences Permanent

But all this misses the point. Today's diversity doctrine was contrived as a means of making racial preferences permanent. After all, affirmative action was intended as a temporary remedy for the tragic mistreatment of blacks. But as affirmative action drifted into racial preferences, it became constitutionally suspect because racial preferences are by definition discriminatory. If I give extra credit to Joe because he's black, I'm making things just that much harder for Tom because he's white.

There was a time when condescension, discrimination, arrogant social engineering along racial lines and the like were dubbed racism.

The brilliance of the diversity doctrine is that it does an end-run around all of this by saying that diversity isn't so much about helping the underprivileged, it's about providing a rich educational experience for everyone.

When the University of Michigan's admissions policies were being reviewed by the Supreme Court, former school president Lee Bollinger explained that diversity was as "as essential as the study of the Middle Ages, of international politics and of Shakespeare" because exposure to people of different hues lies at the core of the educational experience. That's another way of saying that racial preferences are forever, just like the timeless works of the immortal bard. That business about redressing past discrimination against blacks is no longer the name of the game.

It's difficult to put into words how condescending this is in that it renders black students into props, show-and-tell objects for the other kids' educational benefit.

There was a time when condescension, discrimination, arrogant social engineering along racial lines and the like were dubbed racism. And, to paraphrase Shakespeare, racism by any other name still stinks.

CHAPTER 4

What Should Be Done About Racism?

Chapter Preface

Although there is disagreement about the extent of racism in the United States and the severity of the problem, few dispute that racism exists. Given that, the questions arise: what should be done about racism and how can further racial discrimination be prevented? Broadly speaking, there are two camps in this debate: 1) the side that thinks paying no attention to race is the answer; and 2) the side that believes Americans should focus on achieving racial equality, even if that means making decisions based on race to get there. Affirmative action is one kind of proposed solution to racism that has ignited arguments between these two camps. With respect to the issue of school segregation, the two sides also take very different approaches.

One significant issue in the Civil Rights Movement concerned racial segregation in public schools. The U.S. Supreme Court's decision in *Brown v. Board of Education* (1954) declared that state laws establishing separate public schools for black and white students were unconstitutional. After the 1954 *Brown* decision, public schools could no longer legally be segregated, though many remained segregated anyway. A second Supreme Court decision in 1955, known as *Brown II*, mandated that desegregation be carried out "with all deliberate speed." This ruling prompted some desegregation but also led many communities in the South to close down public schools in favor of private schools to avoid having to integrate. More than fifty years later, most public schools are still not racially integrated for a variety of reasons.

Jonathan Kozol, author of *The Shame of the Nation: The Restoration of Apartheid Schooling in America*, claims, "Schools that were already deeply segregated twenty-five or thirty years ago are no less segregated now, while thousands of other schools around the country that had been integrated either voluntarily or by the force of law have since been rapidly re-segregating." Public school districts around the country have dealt with the issue in different ways—some by doing nothing and others by making attempts at some racial integration. A school district in Seattle, Washington, for example, had a policy of using race as a tiebreaker in assigning students to popular high schools. Students would apply to their top choices; if those schools had more applicants than they could accommodate, the district decided who would go where based on race. Proponents of the policy believed that the purpose of the policy—attempting to achieve racial diversity in the school population—justified the use of race in making decisions about public school enrollment. Opponents, however, believed that the policy was an egregious use of racial classification.

The dispute resulted in the U.S. Supreme Court case *Parents Involved in Community Schools v. Seattle School District No. 1* (2007). The Supreme Court sided with the opponents of the policy, ruling that the programs were "directed only to racial balance, pure and simple," a goal Chief Justice John Roberts said was forbidden by the Constitution's guarantee of equal protection. Roberts claimed, "The way to stop discrimination on the basis of race is to stop discriminating on the basis of race." In his dissent, Justice Stephen Breyer expressed concern that "the last half-century has witnessed great strides toward racial equality, but we have not yet realized the promise of *Brown*. To invalidate the plans under review is to threaten the promise of *Brown*." Whereas Breyer believes that policies that take race into account in order to achieve racial equality are still necessary, Roberts believes that such policies constitute racial discrimination. The two views mirror the core disagreement, reflected in the viewpoints of this chapter, in many debates about what should be done to solve the problem of racism.

Whites and Blacks Must Play a Role in Eliminating Racism

Barack Obama

Barack Obama is the forty-fourth president of the United States.

"We the people, in order to form a more perfect union."

Two hundred and twenty one years ago, in a hall that still stands across the street, a group of men gathered and, with these simple words, launched America's improbable experiment in democracy. Farmers and scholars; statesmen and patriots who had traveled across an ocean to escape tyranny and persecution finally made real their declaration of independence at a Philadelphia convention that lasted through the spring of 1787.

The document they produced was eventually signed but ultimately unfinished. It was stained by this nation's original sin of slavery, a question that divided the colonies and brought the convention to a stalemate until the founders chose to allow the slave trade to continue for at least twenty more years, and to leave any final resolution to future generations.

Of course, the answer to the slavery question was already embedded within our Constitution—a Constitution that had at is very core the ideal of equal citizenship under the law; a Constitution that promised its people liberty, and justice, and a union that could be and should be perfected over time.

And yet words on a parchment would not be enough to deliver slaves from bondage, or provide men and women of every color and creed their full rights and obligations as citizens of the United States. What would be needed were Americans in successive generations who were willing to do their part—through protests and struggle, on the streets and in the courts, through a civil war and civil disobedience and always at great risk—to narrow that gap between the promise of our ideals and the reality of their time.

One Out of Many

This was one of the tasks we set forth at the beginning of this campaign [for president in 2008]—to continue the long march of those who came before us, a march for a more just, more equal, more free, more caring and more prosperous America. I chose to run for the presidency at this moment in history because I believe deeply that we cannot solve the challenges of our time unless we solve them together—unless we perfect our union by understanding that we may have different stories, but we hold common hopes; that we may not look the same and we may not have come from the same place, but we all want to move in the same direction—toward a better future for our children and our grandchildren.

This belief comes from my unyielding faith in the decency and generosity of the American people. But it also comes from my own American story.

This nation is more than the sum of its parts . . . out of many, we are truly one.

I am the son of a black man from Kenya and a white woman from Kansas. I was raised with the help of a white grandfather who survived a Depression to serve in Patton's Army during World War II and a white grandmother who worked on a bomber assembly line at Fort Leavenworth while he was overseas. I've gone to some of the best schools in America and lived in one of the world's poorest nations. I am married to a black American who carries within her the blood of slaves and slaveowners—an inheritance we pass on to our two precious daughters. I have brothers, sisters, nieces, nephews, uncles and cousins, of every race and every hue, scattered across three continents, and for as long as I live, I will never forget that in no other country on Earth is my story even possible.

It's a story that hasn't made me the most conventional candidate. But it is a story that has seared into my genetic makeup the idea that this nation is more than the sum of its parts—that out of many, we are truly one.

The Racial Divide

Throughout the first year of this campaign, against all predictions to the contrary, we saw how hungry the American people were for this message of unity. Despite the temptation to view my candidacy through a purely racial lens, we won commanding victories in states with some of the whitest populations in the country. In South Carolina, where the Confederate Flag still flies, we built a powerful coalition of African Americans and white Americans.

This is not to say that race has not been an issue in the campaign. At various stages in the campaign, some commentators have deemed me either "too black" or "not black enough." We saw racial tensions bubble to the surface during the week before the South Carolina primary. The press has scoured every exit poll for the latest evidence of racial polarization, not just in terms of white and black, but black and brown as well.

And yet, it has only been in the last couple of weeks that the discussion of race in this campaign has taken a particularly divisive turn.

On one end of the spectrum, we've heard the implication that my candidacy is somehow an exercise in affirmative action; that it's based solely on the desire of wide-eyed liberals to purchase racial reconciliation on the cheap. On the other end, we've heard my former pastor, Reverend Jeremiah Wright, use incendiary language to express views that have the potential not only to widen the racial divide, but views that denigrate both the greatness and the goodness of our nation; that rightly offend white and black alike. . . .

So many of the disparities that exist in the African-American community today can be directly traced to inequalities passed on from an earlier generation.

The fact is that the comments that have been made and the issues that have surfaced over the last few weeks reflect the complexities of race in this country that we've never really worked through—a part of our union that we have yet to perfect. And if we walk away now, if we simply retreat into our respective corners, we will never be able to come together and solve challenges like health care, or education, or the need to find good jobs for every American.

A History of Inequality

Understanding this reality requires a reminder of how we arrived at this point. As William Faulkner once wrote, "The past isn't dead and buried. In fact, it isn't even past." We do not need to recite here the history of racial injustice in this country. But we do need to remind ourselves that so many of the disparities that exist in the African-American community today can be directly traced to inequalities passed on from an earlier generation that suffered under the brutal legacy of slavery and Jim Crow.

Segregated schools were, and are, inferior schools; we still haven't fixed them, fifty years after *Brown v. Board of Education*, and the inferior education they provided, then and now, helps explain the pervasive achievement gap between today's black and white students.

Legalized discrimination—where blacks were prevented, often through violence, from owning property, or loans were not granted to African-American business owners, or black homeowners could not access FHA [Federal Housing Administration] mortgages, or blacks were excluded from unions, or the police force, or fire departments—meant that black families could not amass any meaningful wealth to bequeath to future generations. That history helps explain the wealth and income gap between black and white, and the concentrated pockets of poverty that persist in so many of today's urban and rural communities.

What's remarkable is not how many failed in the face of discrimination, but rather how many men and women overcame the odds.

A lack of economic opportunity among black men, and the shame and frustration that came from not being able to provide for one's family, contributed to the erosion of black families—a problem that welfare policies for many years may have worsened. And the lack of basic services in so many urban black neighborhoods—parks for kids to play in, police walking the beat, regular garbage pick-up and building code enforcement—all helped create a cycle of violence, blight and neglect that continue to haunt us.

Black Anger

This is the reality in which Reverend Wright and other African-Americans of his generation grew up. They came of age in the late fifties and early sixties, a time when segregation was still the law of the land and opportunity was systematically constricted. What's remarkable is not how many failed in the face of discrimination, but rather how many men and women overcame the odds; how many were able to make a way out of no way for those like me who would come after them.

But for all those who scratched and clawed their way to get a piece of the American Dream, there were many who didn't make it—those who were ultimately defeated, in one way or another, by discrimination. That legacy of defeat was passed on to future generations—those young men and, increasingly, young women whom we see standing on street corners or languishing in our prisons, without hope or prospects for the future. Even for those blacks who did make it, questions of race, and racism, continue to define their worldview in fundamental ways. For the men and women of Reverend Wright's generation, the memories of humiliation and doubt and fear have not gone away; nor has the anger and the bitterness of those years. That anger may not get expressed in public, in front of white co-workers or white friends. But it does find voice in the barbershop or around the kitchen table. At times, that anger is exploited by politicians, to gin up votes along racial lines, or to make up for a politician's own failings.

Most working- and middle-class white Americans don't feel that they have been particularly privileged by their race.

And occasionally it finds voice in the church on Sunday morning, in the pulpit and in the pews. The fact that so many people are surprised to hear that anger in some of Reverend Wright's sermons simply reminds us of the old truism that the most segregated hour in American life occurs on Sunday morning. That anger is not always productive; indeed, all too often it distracts attention from solving real problems; it keeps us from squarely facing our own complicity in our condition, and prevents the African-American community from forging the alliances it needs to bring about real change. But the anger is real; it is powerful; and to simply wish it away, to condemn it without understanding its roots, only serves to widen the chasm of misunderstanding that exists between the races.

White Anger

In fact, a similar anger exists within segments of the white community. Most working- and middle-class white Americans don't feel that they have been particularly privileged by their race. Their experience is the immigrant experience—as far as they're concerned, no one's handed them anything, they've built it from scratch. They've worked hard all their lives, many times only to see their jobs shipped overseas or their pension dumped after a lifetime of labor. They are anxious about their futures, and feel their dreams slipping away; in an era of stagnant wages and global competition, opportunity comes to be seen as a zero sum game, in which your dreams come at my expense. So when they are told to bus their children to a school across town; when they hear that an African American is getting an advantage in landing a good job or a spot in a good college because of an injustice that they themselves never committed; when they're told that their fears about crime in urban neighborhoods are somehow prejudiced, resentment builds over time.

Working together we can move beyond some of our old racial wounds.

Like the anger within the black community, these resentments aren't always expressed in polite company. But they have helped shape the political landscape for at least a generation. Anger over welfare and affirmative action helped forge the [Ronald] Reagan Coalition. Politicians routinely exploited fears of crime for their own electoral ends. Talk show hosts and conservative commentators built entire careers unmasking bogus claims of racism while dismissing legitimate discussions of racial injustice and inequality as mere political correctness or reverse racism.

Just as black anger often proved counterproductive, so have these white resentments distracted attention from the real culprits of the middle class squeeze—a corporate culture rife with inside dealing, questionable accounting practices, and short-term greed; a Washington dominated by lobbyists and special interests; economic policies that favor the few over the many. And yet, to wish away the resentments of white Americans, to label them as misguided or even racist, without recognizing they are grounded in legitimate concerns—this too widens the racial divide, and blocks the path to understanding.

Working Together

This is where we are right now. It's a racial stalemate we've been stuck in for years. Contrary to the claims of some of my critics, black and white, I have never been so naïve as to believe that we can get beyond our racial divisions in a single election cycle, or with a single candidacy—particularly a candidacy as imperfect as my own.

But I have asserted a firm conviction—a conviction rooted in my faith in God and my faith in the American people— that working together we can move beyond some of our old racial wounds, and that in fact we have no choice if we are to continue on the path of a more perfect union.

For the African-American community, that path means embracing the burdens of our past without becoming victims of our past. It means continuing to insist on a full measure of justice in every aspect of American life. But it also means binding our particular grievances—for better health care, and better schools, and better jobs—to the larger aspirations of all Americans—the white woman struggling to break the glass ceiling, the white man whose been laid off, the immigrant trying to feed his family. And it means taking full responsibility for own lives—by demanding more from our fathers, and spending more time with our children, and reading to them, and teaching them that while they may face challenges and discrimination in their own lives, they must never succumb to despair or cynicism; they must always believe that they can write their own destiny.

Ironically, this quintessentially American—and yes, conservative—notion of self-help found frequent expression in Reverend Wright's sermons. But what my former pastor too often failed to understand is that embarking on a program of self-help also requires a belief that society can change.

The profound mistake of Reverend Wright's sermons is not that he spoke about racism in our society. It's that he spoke as if our society was static; as if no progress has been made; as if this country—a country that has made it possible for one of his own members to run for the highest office in the land and build a coalition of white and black; Latino and Asian, rich and poor, young and old—is still irrevocably bound to a tragic past. But what we know—what we have seen—is that America can change. That is true genius of this nation. What we have already achieved gives us hope—the audacity to hope—for what we can and must achieve tomorrow.

This union may never be perfect, but generation after generation has shown that it can always be perfected.

In the white community, the path to a more perfect union means acknowledging that what ails the African-American community does not just exist in the minds of black people; that the legacy of discrimination—and current incidents of discrimination, while less overt than in the past—are real and must be addressed. Not just with words, but with deeds—by investing in our schools and our communities; by enforcing our civil rights laws and ensuring fairness in our criminal justice system; by providing this generation with ladders of opportunity that were unavailable for previous generations. It requires all Americans to realize that your dreams do not have to come at the expense of my dreams; that investing in the health, welfare, and education of black and brown and white children will ultimately help all of America prosper.

In the end, then, what is called for is nothing more, and nothing less, than what all the world's great religions demand—that we do unto others as we would have them do unto us. Let us be our brother's keeper, Scripture tells us. Let us be our sister's keeper. Let us find that common stake we all have in one another, and let our politics reflect that spirit as well. . . .

I would not be running for President if I didn't believe with all my heart that this is what the vast majority of Americans want for this country. This union may never be perfect, but generation after generation has shown that it can always be perfected. And today, whenever I find myself feeling doubtful or cynical about this possibility, what gives me the most hope is the next generation—the young people whose attitudes and beliefs and openness to change have already made history in this election.

Acknowledging Feelings About Race Is a Necessary Step to Ending Racism

Bryan N. Massingale

Bryan N. Massingale is associate professor of theology at Marquette University, a Jesuit Catholic university.

At Marquette University, where I am a theology professor, I teach the course "Christian and Racial Justice." Over the course of the semester, I ask the students, "What are you feeling?" I have realized that discussions of race cause deep emotions to well up, which, if not acknowledged, impede intellectual engagement with the material we are studying. I note each emotion as it is called out: fear, anger, confusion, resentment, guilt, helplessness, shame, outrage, despair, resignation.

I then give them the following reassurance and challenge: "What you are feeling is perfectly normal. We are dealing with difficult stuff. These emotions are to be expected. But we don't have to be controlled by them. Acknowledge what you are feeling. But remember, you don't have to act out of what you are feeling." That reassurance and clearing the air is often what is needed for us to engage once again in the tasks at hand.

Exploring the Nonrational

My point is simple but often overlooked: Discussions of race and racism engage us at a gut level, stirring up fears and anxieties of which we are often unaware. And unless these are acknowledged in some way, no reasonable discussion of race and racial injustice is possible. Racism cannot be resolved by

Bryan N. Massingale, "Race, Racism Engage Us at Gut Level," *National Catholic Reporter*, vol. 44, no. 16, April 4, 2008, p. 5. Copyright © The National Catholic Reporter Publishing Company, 115 E. Armour Blvd., Kansas City, MO 64111. All rights reserved. Reproduced by permission of National Catholic Reporter, www.natcath.org.

rational appeals or intellectual debates alone. We have to contend with what Martin Luther King Jr. called the "nonrational barriers" that hinder racial unity.

This insight affords a perspective for understanding the widespread unease caused by some incendiary remarks spoken by the [Reverend] Jeremiah Wright, the former pastor of the church attended by Barack Obama.

Rationally, one would think that Obama's repeated denunciations, direct condemnations and emphatic repudiations of this pastor's rhetoric would have been enough to quash the issue, and we would have moved on.

For what religious person hasn't heard a priest, minister or rabbi utter from the pulpit boneheaded, ill-advised, insensitive, embarrassing or even stupid statements that offended common sense and even one's religious convictions? And yet decided that because the church's merits outweighed the minister's shortcomings, one could remain a member of the congregation? Who among us would want to be held responsible for every pronouncement made by our faith's leaders?

The fact that many seem unable to grasp these points is a signal that something more is fueling this ongoing discussion. And until we name it, we won't be able to move beyond it.

Racism cannot be resolved by rational appeals or intellectual debates alone.

The Fear

I suspect that an underlying issue is this: Obama's association with Wright raises a visceral fear in many whites that Obama may be another "angry black man." They dread that he may be a closet Al Sharpton, a secret Louis Farrakhan, a stealth advocate of racial hostility, an undercover agent for racial "payback."

This sounds absurd, even preposterous when put so directly. But race-based anxieties are not rational, and this would not be the first time that racial absurdity has affected the public discourse of Obama's candidacy. How else would one characterize discussions such as: "Is Obama black enough?" or, "Is he too black?" or "Why are 'all the blacks' voting for him?" (disregarding the reality that he couldn't have carried Wisconsin—not to mention Iowa, Utah, and Idaho—with only the black vote)?

Because most whites know few if any black men in any depth, the Wright controversy causes many to view Obama through the filter of "black men" that has been constructed for them. They see him through the lens of what they have heard—and fear—about black men. Obama thus becomes not a black individual, but an entity based upon a composite of the few political black men whom whites "know" through the media. Men like Sharpton, Farrakhan and Jesse Jackson. This is not rational, but it is real.

What is happening to Obama is a common experience for many black men. He has become a walking "ink-blot," a living Rorschach test upon which white fears, fantasies and anxieties are projected.

As a black man who is also a Catholic priest, I am familiar with this dynamic. Well-intentioned white parishioners have told me after a service that I remind them of Denzel Washington (though I wish I were that handsome), Clarence Thomas (though I hold political views that are the polar opposite of his), and Jesse Jackson (though I could never match his rhetorical riffs). I am seen through the prism of the only black men they "know."

I have also been told by well-meaning whites that I am "too soft on race" (that is, not black enough), while others have written that I am nothing more than a "race hustler" (that is, too black). I have had a white coworker, a good friend, run from me in fear as I approached her at dusk wearing a baseball cap and without my identifying collar. I have come to realize that for many, without their conscious awareness, I am a living Rorschach inkblot upon which they read their own unexamined concerns, fears and anxieties.

Interracial love is a cure for racial domination, not its incubator.

This is one of the deepest tragedies of racism or any social prejudice: It robs one of the freedom to be an individual—to be "me"—rather than a "category" (for example, "angry black man" or "racial assimilationist").

I am not arguing that the choice is to support Obama or be considered a racist. My point is that we have to be aware of the latent fears—fears that could be deliberately exploited—that may skew our view of him.

The Power of Love

Whatever shortcomings Obama may have or whatever our political disagreements with him, at least let us understand that he is not a stealth agent for black supremacy. He couldn't be for a simple reason: He has been intimately shaped, influenced and loved by his mother, grandfather, and grandmother—all of whom were white. He loves, and is loved by, both white individuals and black persons in a way that few Americans can ever understand or will ever experience. Interracial love is a cure for racial domination, not its incubator.

In the New Testament, it is written, "There is no fear in love. Perfect love casts out fear." In my classroom, I have witnessed the transformative power of love. My experience teaching about racial justice shows that when people are able to confront their fears and anxieties with understanding and without condemnation, they can move beyond them. We can't help how we feel, but we can decide not to be controlled by our feelings.

Love is what fuels Obama's hope that Americans can move beyond our visceral fears to end what he calls our "racial stalemate." It is up to us to demonstrate whether we are worthy of such trust.

Having a Black President Will Help to Eliminate Racism

Alvin Poussaint, interviewed by CNN

Alvin Poussaint is professor of psychiatry at Harvard Medical School and coauthor with Bill Cosby of Come on People: On the Path from Victims to Victors. *CNN is a leading news network.*

Rev. Martin Luther King Jr. told followers the night before he was killed that he had been "to the mountaintop" and seen the promised land of racial equality. [The] election of Barack Obama was the equivalent of taking all African-Americans to that peak, says Dr. Alvin Poussaint.

In his view, Obama's victory wasn't just a political triumph. It was a seismic event in the history of black America.

Poussaint has made it his life's work to study how African-Americans see themselves and how the larger society sees them.

From the days of the civil rights movement through the 1980s, when he was a script consultant on "The Cosby Show," to today, he has been a leader in assessing how images of black people in the media shape perceptions. Poussaint, who is 74, is professor of psychiatry at Judge Baker Children's Center in Boston and at Harvard Medical School.

At a key point in the civil rights movement, Poussaint moved to Mississippi and worked for the Medical Committee for Human Rights, in Jackson, from 1965 to 1967, helping care for civil rights workers and aiding the desegregation of hospitals and other health care institutions.

Interview with Alvin Poussaint, "Commentary: Obama, Cosby, King, and the Mountaintop," *CNN*, November 13, 2008. www.cnn.com. Copyright © 2008 *CNN*. All rights reserved. Reproduced by permission.

Poussaint met Bill Cosby in the 1970s and has worked with him on a variety of books and shows, most recently co-authoring a book with Cosby. He was interviewed by CNN [in November 2008].

The First Black President

CNN: What do you think is the long-term impact of the election of Barack Obama as a symbol and a message to the black community in America?

Alvin Poussaint: We're going to have a generation of children—if he's in there for eight years—being born in 2009, looking at television and images, hearing before they can talk, absorbing it in their brain and being wired to see the visual images of a black man being president of the United States and understanding very early that that's the highest position in the United States.

So I think that's going to be very powerful in its visual imagery . . . and they're going to see these images constantly on television, probably offsetting a lot of the negative imagery that they may see in shows and videos and sometimes in stereotypic comedy.

These images will also make black parents proud. Although there are many barriers to this, it might put back on the table the importance of the two-parent family. . . . Maybe it will do something for couples and bring black men and black women closer together.

The sense of pride may carry over into family life, the same way it is being carried over now into the life of the church already. At black churches this past Sunday, all of them were talking about Obama and being ambassadors for Obama—in other words, suggesting that now that he's president, that black people should take the high road.

The big problem with all of this is that if there's high expectations that somehow the social ills that the black community faces will suddenly evaporate, they're going to be disappointed—because the economy, the economic crisis is a major issue that's going to affect the black community, making things worse.... So there's going to be more unemployment, more poor people, more black homeless and more poverty....

Maybe more blacks will break through the glass ceiling in corporations, more blacks may, because of their new-found confidence, become more civically engaged, run for office.

Obama's also going to have a positive effect on the white community. Way back in the 1960s, I used to go to Atlanta when it was segregated and even after it started desegregating. When you went downtown to restaurants, you would walk in as a black person and they would kind of act like, "What are you doing here?" You weren't welcome, you know, you just felt it.

And Maynard Jackson became the first black mayor, and I felt a whole change in the tone of the city. You went places and when you walked in, people had to consider: "Is this someone who knows the mayor, this black person?" And so I think they began to treat all black people better because black people were now in power.... This may help to eradicate stereotypes that they hold....

So this may have a spinoff effect—maybe more blacks will break through the glass ceiling in corporations, more blacks may, because of their newfound confidence, become more civically engaged, run for office.

What if he had lost, what would the impact have been then?

A lot of black people would have concluded that he lost because of his race, and the black people who had no faith in the system in the first place would have continued to feel that way, maybe even more strongly, and maybe even have more anger at the institutions that have authority over them and that they see as white-controlled.

Obama is taking over at a time of tremendous international and national challenges. Every president has setbacks. What would be the impact of setbacks on a political level?

Nearly everybody that you hear talk about it realizes that he's inheriting a horrible situation. In fact one of the black leaders joked about how, as soon as things are falling apart in the country, that they hand it over to a black person—"Here, you take it."

There's a mindset right now of "What can we do to help Obama?"

People are saying that he's just been dealt a terrible hand and is going to have to work very hard to be successful and they're rooting for him and hoping. There's a mindset right now of "What can we do to help Obama?" And I don't think it's just black people saying it, it's all the people who voted for him, young people and women, the workers, the unions— "What can we do to help him be successful, and undo the mess that we're in?"

The Cosby Show

What do you make of the idea that The Cosby Show *made America more ready to vote for a black man to be president?*

I don't know, you can't study this stuff scientifically. The intent when *The Cosby Show* came on . . . was to present a black family that was not the old stereotypical family that white people laughed at in a sitcom. And we wanted the show to have a universality, in terms of a mother, a father, wonderful children, a lot of love being shown, an emphasis on education.

Today if you have 12 or 15 million viewers of a show a week, it's number one. Well, *Cosby* was bringing in about 60 million people a week. So this had a deep effect on white children, Latino children, and even many adults, what their images of black people were.

So that's why [President George W. Bush's adviser] Karl Rove reached into the hat the other day and said this was the beginning of the post-racial era, because it made white people embrace this black family like a family of their own and fall in love with it.

It probably played some role at chipping away at those negative images, which made white people . . . more ready to embrace a lot of things, including Tiger Woods and Oprah Winfrey and Denzel Washington and Will Smith. Certainly when Obama gets on the scene, people don't say, "What kind of black family is that? We haven't seen any black family like that."

Because that's what they said about *The Cosby Show* . . . that this doesn't represent a black family, this is fantasy. And it wasn't fantasy, because there were black families like that in 1984, and there are many more black families like that in the middle class and upper-middle class today.

You were a consultant on The Cosby Show. *How did that come about?*

I knew him and his wife. When the show was coming on, he called me and said he wanted me to . . . be a production consultant to keep this a positive show without stereotyping: "I want you to read and critique every single script before it goes into production, anything you want to say to make this family psychologically believable, living in reality." He wanted the story lines to have a plot that made sense. . . . He told me to weed out what he called put-down humor, which he felt was too prevalent, particularly on a lot of black shows where you make fun of people.

I was allowed to comment on anything, from the clothes to some of the people they were casting, to making sure there was a wide range of colors on the show in terms of complexion, what's on the reading table, what cultural activities the kids are going to, what colleges they're applying to. . . .

Obama's Victory

You co-authored a book with Bill Cosby. What's the message of that book?

It's called, *Come on People: On the Road from Victims to Victors.* The message is, don't be helpless and hopeless and see yourself as a victim and wallow in failing and think that's your lot in life. What you have to do is take the high road and you have to work hard to try to achieve against the odds. . . .

Most of the black people are where they are today because we succeeded against the odds, we didn't allow the racism out there to totally squelch us. And we feel that spirit is being lost, particularly in low-income communities and sometimes among middle-income people too. And we felt they had to adopt more of an attitude of being victors.

And victors are active, they try to do their best, they take education very seriously. And Obama's a good example—if he took a victim's attitude and said, "Well, a black man could never get elected president of the United States," which a lot of us felt like, he wouldn't have run for the presidency. So he adopted what we call a victor's attitude—"I'm going to go for it, it may be a longshot, but it's possible."

What do you compare the Obama victory to in terms of significance?

Obama represents us winning our freedom—like "free at last, free at last, free at last."

The civil rights movement's success in getting the civil rights bill of '64 and the Voting Rights Act of '65, that opened things mightily for the black communities all over the country. Obviously getting those bills and those accomplishments—

forget about *The Cosby Show*—the voting rights bill played a significant role in Obama's victory.

Does Obama's victory as a historical moment equal those?

It equals those but it has a more powerful visual symbolism. It's like people are going from [Martin Luther] King, who was moving us toward the mountaintop . . . to Obama, people saying [we're] getting to the mountaintop and now being able to gaze down. So it's the fruition of a movement beginning in slavery. . . . We were in slavery for 250 years, and then Jim Crow segregation for another 100, and we've been struggling for freedom. Obama represents us winning our freedom—like "free at last, free at last, free at last."

But it's not really true. We still have racial discrimination in the country, we're still going to have racial injustice that we have to work on and eradicate. But he's a great symbol that we're going to get there. We're going to get there.

Having a Black President Will Not Eliminate Racism

Shelby Steele

Shelby Steele is a research fellow at the Hoover Institution at Stanford University and the author of A Bound Man: Why We Are Excited About Obama and Why He Can't Win.

For the first time in human history, a largely white nation has elected a black man to be its paramount leader. And the cultural meaning of this unprecedented convergence of dark skin and ultimate power will likely become—at least for a time—a national obsession. In fact, the [Barack] Obama presidency will always be read as an allegory. Already we are as curious about the cultural significance of his victory as we are about its political significance.

A Post-racial America?

Does his victory mean that America is now officially beyond racism? Does it finally complete the work of the civil rights movement so that racism is at last dismissible as an explanation of black difficulty? Can the good Revs. [Jesse] Jackson and [Al] Sharpton now safely retire to the seashore? Will the Obama victory dispel the twin stigmas that have tormented black and white Americans for so long—that blacks are inherently inferior and whites inherently racist? Doesn't a black in the Oval Office put the lie to both black inferiority and white racism? Doesn't it imply a "post-racial" America? And shouldn't those of us—white and black—who did not vote for Mr. Obama take pride in what his victory says about our culture even as we mourn our political loss?

Answering no to such questions is like saying no to any idealism; it seems callow. How could a decent person not

Shelby Steele, "Obama's Post-Racial Promise," *Los Angeles Times*, November 5, 2008, p. A31. Copyright © 2008 Los Angeles Times. Reproduced by permission of the author.

hope for all these possibilities, or not give America credit for electing its first black president? And yet an element of Barack Obama's success was always his use of the idealism implied in these questions as political muscle. His talent was to project an idealized vision of a post-racial America—and then to have that vision define political decency. Thus, a failure to support Obama politically implied a failure of decency.

Obama's special charisma—since his famous 2004 convention speech—always came much more from the racial idealism he embodied than from his political ideas. In fact, this was his *only* true political originality. On the level of public policy, he was quite unremarkable. His economics were the redistributive axioms of old-fashioned Keynesianism; his social thought was recycled Great Society. But all this policy boilerplate was freshened up—given an air of "change"—by the dreamy post-racial and post-ideological kitsch he dressed it in.

This worked politically for Obama because it tapped into a deep longing in American life—the longing on the part of whites to escape the stigma of racism. In running for the presidency—and presenting himself to a majority white nation—Obama knew intuitively that he was dealing with a stigmatized people. He knew whites were stigmatized as being prejudiced, and that they hated this situation and literally longed for ways to disprove the stigma.

Bargaining with Race

Obama is what I have called a "bargainer"—a black who says to whites, "I will never presume that you are racist if you will not hold my race against me." Whites become enthralled with bargainers out of gratitude for the presumption of innocence they offer. Bargainers relieve their anxiety about being white and, for this gift of trust, bargainers are often rewarded with a kind of halo.

Obama's post-racial idealism told whites the one thing they most wanted to hear: America had essentially contained the evil of racism to the point at which it was no longer a serious barrier to black advancement. Thus, whites became enchanted enough with Obama to become his political base. It was Iowa—95% white—that made him a contender. Blacks came his way only after he won enough white voters to be a plausible candidate.

When whites . . . proudly support Obama for his post-racialism, they unwittingly embrace race as their primary motivation.

Of course, it is true that white America has made great progress in curbing racism over the last 40 years. I believe, for example, that Colin Powell might well have been elected president in 1996 had he run against a then rather weak Bill Clinton. It is exactly because America has made such dramatic racial progress that whites today chafe so under the racist stigma. So I don't think whites really want change from Obama as much as they want documentation of change that has already occurred. They want him in the White House first of all as evidence, certification and recognition.

But there is an inherent contradiction in all this. When whites—especially today's younger generation—proudly support Obama for his post-racialism, they unwittingly embrace race as their primary motivation. They think and act racially, not post-racially. The point is that a post-racial society is a bargainer's ploy: It seduces whites with a vision of their racial innocence precisely to coerce them into acting out of a racial motivation. A real post-racialist could not be bargained with and would not care about displaying or documenting his racial innocence. Such a person would evaluate Obama politically rather than culturally.

Certainly things other than bargaining account for Obama's victory. He was a talented campaigner. He was reassuringly articulate on many issues—a quality that Americans now long for in a president. And, in these last weeks, he was clearly pushed over the top by the economic terrors that beset the nation. But it was the peculiar cultural manipulation of racial bargaining that brought him to the political dance. It inflated him as a candidate, and it may well inflate him as a president.

There is nothing to suggest that Obama will lead America into true post-racialism. His campaign style revealed a tweaker of the status quo, not a revolutionary. Culturally and racially, he is likely to leave America pretty much where he found her.

Disparity will continue to accuse blacks of inferiority and whites of racism ... despite the level of melanin in the president's skin.

Continued Racial Politics

But what about black Americans? Won't an Obama presidency at last lead us across a centuries-old gulf of alienation into the recognition that America really is our country? Might this milestone not infuse black America with a new American nationalism? And wouldn't this be revolutionary in itself? Like most Americans, I would love to see an Obama presidency nudge things in this direction. But the larger reality is the profound disparity between black and white Americans that will persist even under the glow of an Obama presidency. The black illegitimacy rate remains at 70%. Blacks did worse on the SAT in 2000 than in 1990. Fifty-five percent of all federal prisoners are black, though we are only 13% of the population. The academic achievement gap between blacks and whites persists even for the black middle class. All this disparity will continue to accuse blacks of inferiority and whites of racism—thus refueling our racial politics—despite the level of melanin in the president's skin.

The torture of racial conflict in America periodically spits up a new faith that idealism can help us "overcome"—America's favorite racial word. If we can just have the right inspiration, a heroic role model, a symbolism of hope, a new sense of possibility. It is an American cultural habit to endure our racial tensions by periodically alighting on little islands of fresh hope and idealism. But true reform, like the civil rights victories of the '60s, never happens until people become exhausted with their suffering. Then they don't care who the president is.

Presidents follow the culture; they don't lead it. I hope for a competent president.

Color-Blind Idealism Must Be Unmasked as Denial

Patricia J. Williams

Patricia J. Williams is a professor of law at Columbia University Law School and the author of Seeing a Color-Blind Future: The Paradox of Race.

On a short flight to New York recently, I was sitting behind two white, well-dressed twentysomethings chattering loudly and uninhibitedly about going to clubs and travel plans and the possibility of living in New Jersey. Then came the question: "So who are you voting for?"

"I was for Hillary [Clinton], but now . . . I'm kind of undecided," volunteered the first woman.

"Are you a Democrat?" asked the second.

"Yeah. But I think I might go with McCain. It's just that, well, I don't know. You know." Her voice dropped. I leaned forward to hear better. "You kind of hate to say it aloud, but . . ." Here her voice dropped again, to a murmur lost in the roar of the jet engines, and I missed whatever came next.

Fear of Race

Let's start with this concession: I have no idea what that young woman actually said. In a perfect world, I suppose that would be the end of the story and I would go back to minding my own business. In the context of contemporary political discourse, however, it did cross my mind that if this conversation were presented on one of those "finish the sentence" cultural-literacy tests, then pretty much every American, of whatever

Patricia J. Williams, "Talking about Not Talking about Race: Why Even the Most Well-Meaning Whites and Blacks Can't Hear Each Other," *New York Magazine*, vol. 41, no. 29, August 18, 2008, pp. 26–27.

creed, color, or class, would have exactly the same guess as to how the woman completed her thought.

I think there's some consensus, in other words, about the one thing in America we really "hate to say" aloud. Yet by refraining from saying audibly that-which-must-not-be-spoken, was the young woman's political choice rendered rational, neutral, pure? Conversely, if I were to spell it out here, would I be the one accused of "playing the race card"?

Race is one topic that's probably even more taboo in polite company than sex.

This is a complicated monkey wrench in our supposedly post-race society. On the one hand, everyone knows that race matters to a greater or lesser degree; on the other, few of us want to admit it. Indeed, race is the one topic that's probably even more taboo in polite company than sex. Yet in the absence of fact or frank conversation, grown people get buried in the kind of whispered fear, fantasy, and ignorant mistake that a 5-year-old makes when explaining how icky it was when Daddy got Mommy pregnant using the garden hose and a large bowl of avocados. Is this misinformation really so different from when Fox News and Karl Rove fill in the blanks of those awkward silences with images of the perpetually panty-less Paris Hilton rocking the foundations of our civilization on the same stage as Barack *Hussein* Osama, oops, I mean Obama. This is racial pornography that exploits the barely suppressed caverns of imagined horrors that have haunted us since D.W. Griffith's *The Birth of a Nation*.

Obama predicted this phenomenon and attempted to expose it to the anodyne of common sense: "They're going to try to make you afraid of me. 'He's young and inexperienced and he's got a funny name. And did I mention he's black?'" The not-altogether-surprising backlash from McCain's campaign is a deflection, an expression of deep discomfort. The reflexive accusation that Obama was playing the race card has a certain resemblance to the juvenile retort one gets when the science teacher tries to explain the human reproductive system: "Ooooh! He said a dirty word!" In this way, the opportunity for thoughtful public analysis sinks, once again, below the sound of the audible. Yet the fear of race rolls on, pantomimed in palpably influential and consequential ways.

Seeing Racism

At the same time, the civil-rights movement has given us a moral conscience that was not as prevalent when *The Birth of a Nation* was made. Today, it's fair to say that the overwhelming majority of white Americans "hate to say it aloud" because they also hate to think of themselves as racists. But blacks and whites tend to differ in their very definition of racism. Some years ago, researchers conducting a study for the Diversity Project, at UC [University of California] Berkeley's Institute for the Study of Social Change, asked black and white college students about their perceptions of racism on a given campus. White students tended to say there was none, but blacks and Native Americans said it was everywhere. In fact, the study documented an interesting phenomenon: As Diversity Project sociologist Troy Duster put it, "White students see diversity as a potential source of 'individual enhancement,'" while African-American students were more likely to see the goal as "institutional change."

When the white students were asked to give illustrations that substantiated their positions, they spoke of their own experiences and of personal intentions. "Last night, I had dinner with a black friend," they might offer. Or, "I have a black roommate, and we get along"; "I play basketball with a couple of black guys"; "I've never used a racist epithet"; "I treat everyone the same."

The black students cited instances of relative privilege, things that were more structural, institutional, atmospheric.

"The campus police are always stopping us"; "I get followed around in stores"; "Most of the white students don't have to think twice about how much it costs to take prep classes for the LSAT or to spend spring break skiing in Aspen or partying in Cancún."

It's a familiar, even ubiquitous, miscommunication over the last ten years of the so-called culture wars: A black person speaks of racism or white privilege. The nearest halfway-privileged white person protests, "But I work for liberal causes. You're lumping me with racists just because I'm white!"

The tendency to turn the commitment to racial liberalism into sheer denial is strong.

The black person answers, "I'm not saying that you, personally, are a racist. I'm saying we live in a world where it's easier to be white than it is to be black."

"But I'm not part of that," comes the reply.

"We're all part of it," insists the black person.

The tendency to turn the commitment to racial liberalism into sheer denial is strong. "I don't see race" becomes "I don't see racism." But while some of us are listening to the soothing tones of National Public Radio, a much larger audience—and larger by millions—is listening to Rush Limbaugh singing those subterranean fears of "Barack, the magic Negro," or to radio shock jocks cackling about "jigaboos," or to Pat Buchanan fretting that Obama is a radical, unpatriotic, extremist "elitist" to whom the liberal media hands a pass as a "special-ed," "affirmative-action" candidate. Not that any of them mean it in a racist way. Hey, lighten up. Don't you have a sense of humor?

The Reality of Race

Then there are the real-life, on-the-ground, disastrous statistical disparities that burden the lived experience of the majority of blacks, people of color, and the poor in this country: from the still-unrepaired wake of Hurricane Katrina, to the greater infant-mortality rate and lesser life span, to near double-digit rates of unemployment, to CUNY [City University of New York] professor Harry Levine's study of stop-and-frisk statistics in New York City (blacks are eight times more likely than whites to be stopped for marijuana possession, for instance), to disproportionately high national rates of foreclosures and homelessness among blacks, Native Americans, and Latinos, to the almost complete resegregation of schools across the land, to a war on drugs so shockingly racialized and so aggressively executed that our rates of incarceration place us first in the world.

There is an interesting kind of cognitive dissonance at work in the American psyche. We rejoice in the warm symbolism of interracial bliss, particularly in the idealized and thoroughly mythic sphere of celebrity existence: Tiger Woods's Pan-racialism, Brangelina's [Brad Pitt and Angelina Jolie's] adoptions, Steven Spielberg's handsome brown son. We tell ourselves we love the idea of diasporic enfoldment: bi-, tri-, and multiracial Kids 'R' Us. At the same time, there's terrible ambivalence on the ground. Does one really want "the race card" living next door, or being your boss? Do you *really* want your child marrying outside his race? I've had conversations with white friends who are rattled when a black classmate has bested their child in class rank but still can't let go of the feeling that the mere presence of blacks in the school must be bringing down the test scores.

Similarly, it's interesting to review the evolution of media commentary, from TV to the blogosphere, trying to fit the thoroughly unfamiliar Obama into familiar boxes. For a while, he was depicted as not having any "racial baggage." Then, in the blink of an eye, he was transformed into Exactly the Same Person As the Reverend [Jeremiah] Wright—who then could be demonized with all the well-practiced repertoire of insults reserved for [black activist] Louis Farrakhan and armed revolutionaries.

Obama's comeback, his eloquent speech about race, showed that he wasn't exactly the same person, not by any means. So in yet another twist, he is now so uppity he needs bringing down, defamed as too famous, categorized as uncategorizable, displaced as unplaceable. Since, in actuality, more is on the record about every step of Obama's life than possibly any candidate on the planet, this particular brand of demonization has been accomplished by the insinuations of erasure: If you took away his "pretty words," he'd be nothing. If you took away his race, he'd be nothing. If only he didn't have a brain, he'd be nothing, nothing, nothing. It's a circular, nonsensical mantra—magical thinking, wrapped in the fiction of "but really, I never see race." This kind of denial masquerading as color-blind idealism cannot be our compass at this exciting and potentially transformative moment.

To End Racism, Stop Focusing on Race

Kevin Leininger

Kevin Leininger is a columnist for The News-Sentinel, *a Fort Wayne, Indiana, newspaper.*

Swastikas and Ku Klux Klan symbols emblazoned on minority students' lockers. "N----r go home" scribbled on an eighth-grader's seat.

Clearly, Heritage Junior-Senior High School [in Indiana] has a race-relations problem.

At least it did in 1995 when *The News-Sentinel* reported the incidents I just described. It still does, if recent headlines are any indication.

Failed Solutions

But if the persistent lack of civility is an indictment of Heritage and East Allen County Schools [EACS] officials—and it is—it should also give pause to those who believe, contrary to human nature and all evidence, that racism can be eradicated by dividing ourselves into groups, celebrating that diversity and then singing a few rounds of "Kumbaya" around a multicultural campfire.

In other words, the Heritage students threatened simply because of the color of their skin deserve better than the predictable "racism is bad and we've got to do something about it" response. If the goal is to change how teen-agers think, the future will be little different than the past.

EACS Superintendent Kay Novotny knows anything she says about the Heritage incident can be misconstrued and, given the intelligentsia's disdain for the mostly conservative district, probably will be. But she was exactly right when she told me tension often exists in schools dominated by one demographic group—whites in the case of Heritage, where minorities comprise just 10 percent of the 800-student enrollment.

But isn't that an argument for imposing racial balance in the schools, which EACS has steadfastly refused to do over the years because it could lead to consolidation of schools?

Not necessarily. The massively expensive racial-balance program in Fort Wayne Community Schools hasn't ended racial tensions, officials say. And EACS' Southwick Elementary School in southeast Fort Wayne—where whites are in the minority—will also get special attention under the district's anti-racism plan announced [in November 2007]. That's because the influx of refugees and new minority groups is adding layers of cultural and religious complexity that did not previously exist.

"This is greater than a school issue. It's a societal issue," Novotny said. "Values, beliefs and cultures change slowly. You don't have to like everyone, but you do have to treat people decently."

Precisely. But that obvious truth is too often drowned out in America's shrill and often-tiresome debate about race. After the 1995 racial unrest at Heritage near Monroeville was followed by similar problems at New Haven High School two years later, EACS instituted daylong workshops for students at all five of its high schools. The approach didn't solve the problem, obviously, but the latest anti-racism plan calls for— you guessed it—still more workshops called "Study Circles" organized by the United Way of Allen County.

Ironic, since the United Way has at times attacked racism in precisely the worst possible way: by inviting individuals with unique viewpoints and experiences to think in terms of group identity and victimization.

Back in 1999, the United Way distributed a document as part of its campaign to promote diversity on the boards of its member agencies. The document defined racism as "the power of one group in society to systematically oppress those of another group based on color." And who has that power? The privileged: According to the document, those with "advantages, rewards or benefits given to those in the dominant group without their asking for them."

The antidote to racism is not to obsess about race, but to render it irrelevant.

But racism is not defined by power or privilege. To paraphrase Dr. [Martin Luther] King, racism is defined by the unwillingness to judge people by the content of their character, not the color of their skin.

Colorblind Courtesy

The antidote to racism is not to obsess about race, but to render it irrelevant. Instead, many of the same people who have sanctimoniously criticized EACS' handling of the Heritage incident have been vocal proponents of various race-conscious social policies, thereby perpetuating what they profess to despise. If it is OK to group people by race for supposedly benign reasons, why should it surprise anyone when they are done so in a hateful way?

If the racist miscreants at Heritage are identified—and Novotny said 100 investigatory interviews have already been conducted—they deserve to be severely punished and possibly expelled as a warning to others. Not because of what they thought, but because of the thoughtless cruelty of what they did.

Do to others as you would have them do to you. It doesn't earn headlines or require specially trained facilitators. But the

Golden Rule is still good advice, because courtesy should and can be colorblind—even when we're not.

Start there; perhaps understanding and friendship will follow.

To Fight Racism Whites Need to Recognize Their Privilege

Jon Nilson, interviewed by U.S. Catholic

Jon Nilson is a professor of theology at Loyola University–Chicago and the author of Hearing Past the Pain: Why White Catholic Theologians Need Black Theology. U.S. Catholic *is a monthly magazine aimed at American Catholics.*

A relative of Jon Nilson once implied that the only reason Nilson had been given a scholarship to graduate school at the University of Notre Dame was that he had put in a good word for him. Nilson was completely furious. "I was one of the best prepared people in that entry class!" he shot back.

Today he sees it differently. "We have this myth that everything we accomplish we do alone. That's simply not true." For example, he says, just being white can involve dozens of benefits one may not even realize.

Nilson, a theologian at Loyola University Chicago and author of a forthcoming book from Paulist Press on the topic of racism and theology, got his wake-up call about racism after reading the challenging words of a black theologian friend. After some soul searching, he came to a startling conclusion. As president of the Catholic Theological Society of America, Nilson revealed his discovery in a speech, "Confessions of a white Catholic racist theologian." People are still talking about his title and his message, just as he had intended.

Racism and the Holocaust

U.S. Catholic: You've achieved a certain amount of notoriety as having said that you're a white racist theologian. Why did you feel the need to make that confession?

Interview with Jon Nilson, "Racist Like Me: The Editors Interview Jon Nilson," *U.S. Catholic*, vol. 71, no. 12, December 2006, pp. 24–28. Copyright © 2006 by Claretian Publications. Reproduced by permission.

Jon Nilson: It goes back to an article in an issue of *Theological Studies* on black theology by Sister Jamie Phelps, a black theologian teaching at Loyola at the time. In her article she makes the statement that the silence of white Catholic theologians about racism is comparable to the silence of the German theologians during the Holocaust. I couldn't stop thinking about that line because I had done a lot of reading and teaching about Germans during World War II. I had been asking myself how these Christians could have stood by while these horrors were going on right in their own country.

In effect Jamie was saying that if you're looking for a contemporary analog to the German theologians, look closely in your bathroom mirror. At first I thought maybe this is a rhetorical strategy on her part; she's just trying to alarm us, to engage us in these issues. But I was thinking about it while I was jogging, while I was driving. It wouldn't leave me alone.

I decided I had to find out for myself: I started reading, and I came to the conclusion that in fact it was the truth. James Cone, the father of black theology in this country, calls racism America's original sin. He's absolutely right.

I used to understand racism the way many people understand racism: deliberate, overt forms of speech and action that denigrate people of another race.

At the time I was scheduled to deliver an address at the Catholic Theological Society meeting. I knew I couldn't speak about anything else. I've never been much for the traditionally bland title, so I specifically chose, "Confessions of a white Catholic racist theologian." I meant "confessions" in the same way that Augustine meant his *Confessions*: It's an acknowledgment of responsibility, but it's also praise, meaning I'm grateful to God for Sister Jamie's remark that began to wake me up.

Racism and Racists

How do you understand racism differently now from before?

I used to understand racism the way many people understand racism: deliberate, overt forms of speech and action that denigrate people of another race. It can go as far as cross burnings and lynchings, which are very, very dramatic. But I came to understand that it's far more than that. It's oppression and marginalization, and this oppression and this marginalization goes on simply as a matter of course. It's a part of the common sense of the dominant white majority. For example, do we find it odd that in a city like Chicago, the black presence in something like the *Chicago Tribune* is so minimal?

We don't understand our history, we don't see the way our economy works by marginalizing, oppressing, and keeping African Americans in poverty. We accept a grossly unjust educational system that ties the fate of children to where they happen to live. All this falls under the name of racism.

Do you still consider yourself a racist?

I would say yes. Let me make a comparison. I raised two strong daughters, I'm married to a strong woman, and I have a lot of very good women friends and colleagues. So I think I'm sensitized to issues around the status of women, because through these friendships and through these relationships I'm more able to see situations through the eyes of women.

Insofar that we are racists, it's not because of some sort of deliberate decision that we've taken with respect to African Americans.

I don't have those same kinds of relationships with black people. I have black friends, but they teach at Marquette University or Boston College; we see each other once or twice a year. I don't have the frequent contact that would enable me to see my city, my university, our situation through their eyes in the same way. I live in a 99.9 percent white world. So I suspect yes, in some very significant ways, I am still a racist. Too often I simply accept the status quo as just the way it is.

How did others react to your talk?

They were extraordinarily positive, which heartened me a good deal. It showed me there is a tremendous openness on the part of my white colleagues to these issues.

In other words, insofar that we are racists, it's not because of some sort of deliberate decision that we've taken with respect to African Americans. It's rather that our attitudes and our modes of operation are reflective of the history of this country and the history of this particular church. Most Catholics don't know that history; I didn't know that history.

White Privilege

What about the backlash against so-called political correctness? As in, "Well, you're just a self-hating white liberal and the rest of us are beyond that response." Have you heard that?

No, so maybe I've been too measured in everything I've said so far. I haven't even gotten an angry e-mail or a nasty phone call. If someone tried to put that kind of a tag on me, my response would be: No, I and others thinking along these lines are not self-hating white liberals. We're simply white people who want to be sure that we're living in the real world. The world of white privilege is illusory, insofar as it shields us from the insights and the perspective and the wisdom of other cultural and ethnic traditions, most notably the black tradition. I will not ever truly understand how this society works until and unless I see how it works for African Americans, especially those who are exploited and at the bottom of the ladder. For me it's not a question of nurturing self hate, it's simply wanting to open my eyes.

One of the difficulties here is that there are a good number of white intellectuals who are trying to tell us that racism is a thing of the past, that that war is basically over, except for a few battles here and there, and we're on our way to full equality. I think there's a lot of evidence to show that these people are either dishonest or incompetent. They're trying to lull us into even greater complacency than we're already in.

The term "white privilege" is becoming common in some circles. What do you think about that?

I think the term paints with too broad a brush. It suggests that every white person has a significant step up by virtue of their white skin. However true that might be, it doesn't resonate with the experience of a lot of white people. I think it's more off-putting than engaging.

I prefer to say "white benefits." When I look at my own biography, I can see that I've had a certain set of benefits by virtue of my being white, but those wouldn't necessarily be the same as yours. This idea invites white people to investigate their own biography in that way. That said, I think we may be stuck with the term "white privilege."

White Benefits

So what are some "white benefits"?

One of the best entrés into the issue of white privilege for white people is Peggy McIntosh's classic article, "White privilege: Unpacking the invisible knapsack."

The chief benefit of white privilege is not having to think about race at all.

In this article McIntosh identifies benefits that she enjoys that she is fairly sure her black friends do not enjoy. It includes things like how she can walk into a store and not immediately look around to see if she's going to be followed by somebody who thinks she's there to steal something.

Or, for example, when I'm driving and I get stopped, it's probably because I've been going too fast, not because I'm the wrong color in the wrong neighborhood. If I make a mistake,

I don't have to worry that someone is going to say, "Geez, white people are really stupid—did you hear what Nilson just said?"

I have never, ever worried about how to prepare my children for the insults and the contempt that they might face through no fault of their own. I haven't had to control my rage. The chief benefit of white privilege is not having to think about race at all. You get up in the morning and go about your day. You don't have to sweat it.

There is a remarkable book by Thomas Shapiro, an economist at Brandeis University, called *The Hidden Costs of Being African American* (Oxford). He documents in detail how being African American subjects you to fairly stringent financial disadvantages. Whites are more able than blacks, for instance, to help out their adult children. Parents will provide free babysitting or buy a house and let adult children live there rent-free for a few years.

Shapiro and his investigators interviewed white families at length and documented the ways in which their financial status was the consequence of parental assets accumulated over the course of two or three generations. Yet they still could not convince a lot of these couples that somehow their financial status wasn't the result of their own hard work—which feeds into the great myth of America that we pull ourselves up by our own bootstraps. Over and over again it's been shown this is simply not true. I think for many people it's a blow to their self-esteem that maybe they didn't make it this far all on their own.

White Guilt

Should white people feel guilty about this situation?

I don't think guilt is the appropriate response. I really don't. Without calling for pity or compassion for myself, I do think everybody in this society lives a life that has, in some significant ways, been impoverished because of our racial divisions. Sociologist Joe Feagin in *Racist America* points to the amount of time we spend commuting to get out to the suburbs, the money we spend on gas, the time we are away from our families, so we can get away from the inner city where all those "other people" live.

Rather than guilt, perhaps the best response to all this is sadness, profound sadness for one's self, for each other, sadness that is willing to open myself to the pain that this situation inflicts on us.

Was sadness the emotion that motivated you to this new consciousness of yours? Doesn't guilt work better?

No other group [beside blacks] was brought here in chains or was enslaved for so long.

I think for me it became a matter of personal integrity. Either take on the issue of racism or stop calling myself a white Catholic theologian. Call myself a historian of religion or something, but don't call myself a Christian theologian if I'm ducking the main theological issue of this society. So I guess in the end it wasn't really sadness that motivated me.

Whites and Blacks

Why, when we talk about racism in this country, do we think of the relationship between whites and blacks far more than relationships with other races and ethnic groups?

The perception that other ethnic or racial groups have negotiated the obstacles and moved on better than African Americans implies a comparability between blacks and other ethnic groups that I don't think historically can be sustained. Slavery begins shortly after the appearance of white people on this continent. No other group was brought here in chains or was enslaved for so long, no other group was subjected to legalized forms of slavery after the Civil War when the North withdrew its troops and Reconstruction collapsed.

Even today it's far easier for Asians or Hispanics to inter-marry with whites. There's a higher level of social acceptability, unless you happen to be in the military, because the military has remarkably effective anti-discrimination programs. Whites in the military are ten times more likely to marry an African American than whites not in the military. People say we can't legislate race relations. Of course we can. We can get people to wear seat belts and to stop smoking. I think we can do much better where race is concerned if we really want to, but we don't want to.

What have you learned from this issue that affects your faith?

Two things leap to mind, one very practical and one more theoretical. The practical thing is that I think residential segregation profoundly affects the nature of Catholic life at the parish level. We have many all-white parishes and therefore our most frequent ordinary Catholic experience is already giving us a distorted picture of who we are as a church in this country. I think we need to rethink the parish system so it is not so tied to the social sin of residential segregation.

On a more theoretical level, and with the help of people like James Cone, I've come to believe that the main challenge to Christian faith is not the latest writing by an atheist but rather the tolerance of injustice in this country, mainly racial injustice. Why should anybody believe that Jesus has come to transform our lives and reconcile us to one another, as long as we continue to tolerate these divisions?

Changing the Culture

So what can the church do?

The credibility of the gospel in great part depends upon our church being profoundly countercultural about racism, and I don't think the Catholic Church is. We are far too comfortable with this culture.

A lot of my students are very attracted by the prospect of a church that is countercultural, a church that accurately diagnoses what is going on in this culture, that can recognize why people are suffering and what needs to be done about it. There's something deep in us that wants the church to be a leader in that respect. It's not to say that the other things the church is concerned about aren't important, but if we haven't invested most of our energies in trying to achieve social justice, my God, no wonder it looks like we're butchering the gospel.

We don't know what it would be like not to segregate people by economic class or ethnic background.

It gets to your question before about what makes people change, and I think you're right, maybe sadness doesn't do it, although you put in a strong bid for guilt. The other thing that gets people to change is of course pain: It hurts too much to continue the same way. We have to begin to educate ourselves to the ways in which we are all hurt and damaged by racism. We accept our distorted social situation as normal.

We literally don't know what it would be like to have tension-free interactions with people of all different kinds of races. We don't know what it would be like not to segregate people by economic class or ethnic background. We don't know what it would be like if everybody had a certain floor of economic security so that they could participate in the doings of the neighborhood and their government. We just say, this is the way it is and it's sort of fine.

But think of the work of Joe Feagin: "Look pal, you're losing 45 minutes each way out of your day because you're commuting out of the city to get away from the black people. You're spending all this money on gas and you're away from your family longer." That's just a small indication of the costs that we individually and collectively pay to maintain this crazy system. The more we are shown how we are in pain, the more progress we're likely to make.

White Guilt Does Not Help End Racism

George F. Will

George F. Will is a syndicated columnist and author of One Man's America: The Pleasures and Provocations of Our Singular Nation.

The unbearable boredom occasioned by most of today's talk about race is alleviated by a slender, stunning new book. In *White Guilt*, Shelby Steele, America's most discerning black writer, casts a cool eye on yet another soft bigotry of low expectations—the ruinous "compassion" of a theory of social determinism that reduces blacks to, in Steele's word, "non-individuated" creatures.

The Power of Helplessness

That reduction is the basis of identity politics—you *are* your (racial, ethnic, sexual) group. A pioneer of this politics, which is now considered "progressive," was, Steele says, George Wallace. He, too, insisted that race is destiny.

The dehumanizing denial that blacks have sovereignty over their lives became national policy in 1965, when President Lyndon Johnson [LBJ] said: "You do not take a person who, for years, has been hobbled by chains and liberate him, bring him up to the starting line in a race and then say, 'You are free to compete with all the others.'" This, Steele writes, enunciated a new social morality: No black problem could be defined as largely a black responsibility. If you were black, you could not be expected to carry responsibilities equal to others.'

So, being black conferred "an almost reckless moral authority," a "power of racial privilege." The "power to shame, silence and muscle concessions from the larger society" *was* black power. The demand for equal rights became a demand for "the redistribution of responsibility for black advancement from black to white America, from the 'victims' to the 'guilty.'"

Hence the black militancy's proclaiming "black power" was really an exercise in the power of helplessness. It was an assertion of *white* power—white society's power to "take" (LBJ's telling word) blacks to social equality. Hence "black power" was actually a *denial* of the power of blacks to manage their own escape from an intractable inferiority.

Victim status is a source of endless, sometimes lucrative and always guilt-free leverage over a guilt-ridden society.

White Guilt

"By the mid-sixties," Steele writes, "white guilt was eliciting an entirely new kind of black leadership, not selfless men like [Martin Luther] King who appealed to the nation's moral character but smaller men, bargainers, bluffers and haranguers—not moralists but specialists in moral indignation—who could set up a trade with white guilt." The big invention by these small men was what Steele calls "globalized racism." That idea presumes that "racism is not so much an event in black lives as a *condition* of black life," a product of "impersonal" and "structural" forces. The very invisibility of those forces *proved* their sinister pervasiveness.

The theory of "structural" or "institutional" racism postulates a social determinism that makes all whites and American institutions complicit in a vicious cultural pattern. The theory makes the absence of identifiable adverse events in the lives of individual blacks irrelevant to blacks' claims to victimhood. Victim status is a source of endless, sometimes lucrative and always guilt-free leverage over a guilt-ridden society.

Black students who have never suffered discrimination can, Steele says, enjoy affirmative action "with a new sense of entitlement." As a result, Steele says, "We blacks always experience white guilt as an incentive, almost a command, to somehow exhibit racial woundedness and animus." The result for blacks is "a political identity with no real purpose beyond the manipulation of white guilt."

Black "militants" are actually preaching militant dependency. They have defined justice as making whites feel so guilty that they will take responsibility for black advancement. One casualty of this, Steele says, has been education: "We got remedies pitched at injustices rather than at black academic excellence—school busing, black role models as teachers, black history courses, 'diverse' reading lists, 'Ebonics,' multiculturalism, culturally 'inclusive' classes, standardized tests corrected for racial bias, and so on." Reading, writing and arithmetic? Later. Maybe.

Maybe not. Not if classrooms are suffused with "a foggy academic relativism in which scholastic excellence is associated with elitism, and rote development with repression." Steele, a former professor of English, notes that "inner-city black English diverges more from standard English today than it did in the fifties."

Guilt as Condescension

White guilt, Steele says, is a form of self-congratulation, whereby whites devise "compassionate" policies, the real purpose of which is to show that whites are kind and innocent of racism. The "spiritually withering interventions of needy, morally selfish white people" comfortable with "the cliché of black inferiority" have a price. It is paid by blacks, who are "Sambo-ized."

Strong stuff from a fellow of the Hoover Institution at Stanford who [in 2006] received a Bradley Prize, for which this columnist voted. You can read *White Guilt* in two hours. For years it will be a clarifying lens through which to view the lonely struggle of clear sighted black intellectuals to rescue blacks from a degrading temptation. It is the temptation to profit from the condescension toward blacks that is the core of today's white guilt.

Organizations to Contact

The editors have compiled the following list of organizations concerned with the issues debated in this book. The descriptions are derived from materials provided by the organizations. All have publications or information available for interested readers. The list was compiled on the date of publication of the present volume; the information provided here may change. Readers need to remember that many organizations take several weeks or longer to respond to inquiries.

American-Arab Anti-Discrimination Committee (ADC)
4201 Connecticut Avenue NW, Washington, DC 20008
(202) 244-2990 • fax: (202) 244-3196
e-mail: adc@adc.org
Web site: www.adc.org

The American-Arab Anti-Discrimination Committee is a civil rights organization committed to defending the civil rights of people of Arab descent. The ADC has full-time attorneys in its legal department and works with the government to promote the interests of the community. It publishes a series of issue papers and a number of books, including *Hate Crimes Report 2003–2007*.

American Civil Liberties Union (ACLU)
125 Broad Street, 18th Floor, New York, NY 10004
(212) 549-2500
e-mail: infoaclu@aclu.org
Web site: www.aclu.org

The American Civil Liberties Union is a national organization that works to defend Americans' civil rights as guaranteed in the U.S. Constitution. The ACLU's advocacy includes litigation, community organizing and training, legislative initiatives, and public education to preserve and extend the constitutional rights of people of color. The ACLU publishes the semiannual newsletter *Civil Liberties Alert*, as well as briefing papers, including the report *Turning a Blind Eye to Racial Discrimination in America.*

Amnesty International

5 Penn Plaza, 16th Floor, New York, NY   10001
(212) 807-8400 • fax: (212) 463-9193
e-mail: admin-us@aiusa.org
Web site: www.amnesty.org

Amnesty International is a worldwide movement of people who campaign for internationally recognized human rights for all. Amnesty International is a grassroots activist organization that conducts research and generates action to prevent and end grave abuses of human rights and to demand justice for those whose rights have been violated. Among the publications available on its Web site is the report on the death penalty in the United States, noting concerns about racism: "30 Years of Executions, 30 Years of Wrongs."

Anti-Defamation League (ADL)

823 United Nations Plaza, New York, NY   10017
(212) 885-7700
e-mail: webmaster@adl.org
Web site: www.adl.org

The Anti-Defamation League is an international organization that fights prejudice and extremism. It collects, organizes, and distributes information about anti-Semitism, hate crimes, bigotry, and racism. Its publications include *Global Anti-Semitism: Selected Incidents Around the World in 2008.*

Cato Institute

1000 Massachusetts Avenue NW
Washington, DC   20001-5403
(202) 842-0200 • fax: (202) 842-3490

Web site: www.cato.org

The Cato Institute is a public policy research foundation dedicated to limiting the role of government, protecting individual liberties, and promoting free markets. The institute commissions a variety of publications, including books, monographs, briefing papers, and other studies. Among its publications are the quarterly magazine *Regulation*, the bimonthly *Cato Policy Report*, and articles such as "Keeping Racism Alive."

Citizens' Commission on Civil Rights (CCCR)

2000 M Street NW, Suite 400, Washington, DC   20036
(202) 659-5565 • fax: (202) 223-5302
e-mail: citizens@cccr.org
Web site: www.cccr.org

The Citizens' Commission on Civil Rights is a bipartisan organization that seeks ways to accelerate progress in the area of race relations and on other civil rights issues. The organization monitors the civil rights policies and practices of the federal government and works to influence federal education reform. CCCR publishes reports on affirmative action, desegregation, and civil rights, including *The Erosion of Rights: Declining Civil Rights Enforcement Under the Bush Administration*.

Human Rights Watch (HRW)

350 Fifth Avenue, 34th Floor, New York, NY   10118-3299
(212) 290-4700 • fax: (212) 736-1300
e-mail: hrwnyc@hrw.org
Web site: www.hrw.org

Human Rights Watch is dedicated to protecting the human rights of people around the world. It investigates human rights abuses, educates the public, and works to change policy and practice. Among HRW's numerous publications is the report *Targeting Blacks: Drug Law Enforcement and Race in the United States*.

Leadership Conference on Civil Rights (LCCR)
1629 K Street NW, 10th Floor, Washington, DC   20006
(202) 466-3311
Web site: www.civilrights.org

The Leadership Conference on Civil Rights is a coalition of more than 190 national human rights organizations. Its mission is to promote the enactment and enforcement of effective civil rights legislation and policy. The LCCR publishes the annual *Civil Rights Monitor* and reports, such as *American Dream? American Reality! A Report on Race, Ethnicity, and the Law in the United States*, all available on its Web site.

National Association for the Advancement of Colored People (NAACP)
4805 Mt. Hope Drive, Baltimore, MD   21215
(877) 622-2798 • fax: (202) 463-2953
e-mail: youth@naacpnet.org
Web site: www.naacp.org

The National Association for the Advancement of Colored People aims to ensure the political, educational, social, and economic equality of rights of all persons and to eliminate racial hatred and discrimination. In pursuit of these goals, the NAACP is vocal and active in the media and with government officials and representatives, seeking to influence legislation and public policy. The NAACP publishes the magazine *The Crisis*, as well as a variety of newsletters, books, and pamphlets addressing topics ranging from legal issues to education.

U.S. Commission on Civil Rights (USCCR)
624 Ninth Street NW, Washington, DC   20425
(202) 376-7700
e-mail: publications@usccr.gov
Web site: www.usccr.gov

The U.S. Commission on Civil Rights is the agency of the government charged with investigating complaints of discrimination. In addition to investigating complaints, the commission gathers information related to discrimination, appraises federal laws and policies with respect to discrimination, and submits recommendations to the president and Congress. USCCR publishes the *Civil Rights Journal* and other publications on issues of local and regional concern, including the briefing report, *The Economic Stagnation of the Black Middle Class.*

Bibliography

Books

Eduardo Bonilla-Silva — *Racism Without Racists: Color-Blind Racism and the Persistence of Racial Inequality in the United States.* Lanham, MD: Rowman & Littlefield, 2006.

Justin Akers Chacon and Mike Davis — *No One Is Illegal: Fighting Racism and State Violence on the U.S.-Mexico Border.* Chicago: Haymarket Books, 2006.

Rosalind S. Chou and Joe R. Feagin — *The Myth of the Model Minority: Asian Americans Facing Racism.* Boulder, CO: Paradigm, 2008.

Bill Cosby and Alvin F. Poussaint — *Come On People: On the Path from Victims to Victors.* Nashville: Thomas Nelson, 2007.

Michael Eric Dyson — *Is Bill Cosby Right? Or Has the Black Middle Class Lost Its Mind?* New York: Basic Civitas Books, 2006.

Joe R. Feagin — *Systemic Racism: A Theory of Oppression.* New York: Routledge, 2006.

George M. Fredrickson — *Racism: A Short History.* Princeton, NJ: Princeton University Press, 2003.

Joseph Graves — *The Race Myth: Why We Pretend Race Exists in America.* New York: Plume, 2005.

Robert Jensen — *The Heart of Whiteness: Confronting Race, Racism and White Privilege.* San Francisco: City Lights, 2005.

John McWhorter — *Winning the Race: Beyond the Crisis in Black America.* New York: Gotham, 2006.

Chip Smith — *The Cost of Privilege: Taking On the System of White Supremacy and Racism.* Fayetteville, NC: Camino Press, 2007.

Thomas Sowell — *Black Rednecks and White Liberals.* New York: Encounter Books, 2005.

Shelby Steele — *White Guilt: How Blacks and Whites Together Destroyed the Promise of the Civil Rights Era.* New York: HarperCollins, 2006.

Shannon Sullivan — *Revealing Whiteness: The Unconscious Habits of Racial Privilege.* Bloomington: Indiana University Press, 2006.

Beverly Daniel Tatum — *"Why Are All The Black Kids Sitting Together in the Cafeteria?" And Other Conversations About Race.* New York: Basic Books, 2003.

Barbara Trepagnier — *Silent Racism: How Well-Meaning White People Perpetuate the Racial Divide.* Boulder, CO: Paradigm, 2007.

Tim Wise — *White Like Me: Reflections on Race from a Privileged Son.* New York: Soft Skull Press, 2004.

Periodicals

Stephen L. Carter   "Affirmative Distraction," *New York Times*, July 6, 2008.

Irene Change   "Race Matters," *Working Mother*, June–July 2008.

Linda Chavez   "Unbridled Racism Colors Immigration Debate," *Grand Rapids (MI) Press*, June 3, 2007.

Bill Cosby and Alvin F. Poussaint   "Blacks Must Drop Victimhood and Reclaim Dignity," *Christian Science Monitor*, November 8, 2007.

Ellis Cose   "The Color of Change," *Newsweek*, November 13, 2006.

Brian Darling   "Flying in Unfriendly Skies," The Heritage Foundation, December 8, 2006. www.heritage.org.

Maureen Downey   "Rich White Kids 'Winning War over College Affirmative Action,'" *Atlanta Journal Constitution*, September 2, 2007.

Bruce Fein   "Resurgent Racism," *Washington Times*, March 6, 2007.

Craig Franklin   "Media Myths About the Jena 6," *Christian Science Monitor*, October 24, 2007.

Lawrence E. Harrison   "Could Obama's Rise Signal the End of Black Victimology?" *Christian Science Monitor*, August 6, 2008.

John L. Jackson Jr. — "Racial Paranoia and Jeremiah Wright," *Chronicle of Higher Education*, May 16, 2008.

John B. Judis — "The Big Race," *New Republic*, May 28, 2008.

Eugene Kane — "An Obama Victory Won't End Racism," *Milwaukee Journal Sentinel*, May 11, 2008.

Peter Katel — "Race and Politics: Will Skin Color Influence the Presidential Election?," *CQ Researcher*, July 18, 2008.

Raina Kelley — "Let's Talk About Race," *Newsweek*, December 4, 2006.

Sadiqa Khan — "Going Dutch: Reflections on Nation, Race, and Privilege," *Briarpatch*, August 2008.

Paul Krugman — "It's a Different Country," *New York Times*, June 9, 2008.

Karen V. Lee — "White Whispers," *Qualitative Inquiry*, September 2008.

John Leo — "Katrina Isn't About Race," *Grand Rapids (MI) Press*, September 17, 2005.

John McWhorter — "ObamaKids: And the 10-year-olds Shall Lead Us," *New York*, August 18, 2008.

Roberta Munroe "Race Relations: Is the End of Racism in the Hands of Gay White Men and Their Adopted Black Children?" *Advocate*, August 28, 2007.

Mackubin Thomas Owens "A Mistaken Apology for Slavery," *Christian Science Monitor*, January 11, 2008.

John Perazzo "Obama's Ascendancy and the Myth of 'Racist' America," *FrontPage Magazine*, January 10, 2008. www.frontpagemag.com.

Leonard Pitts Jr. "Slip-up Isn't Same as Racism," *Palm Beach (FL) Post*, January 19, 2008.

Tom Roberts "Confronting White Privilege: Can Today's Politics Shift the Balance?" *National Catholic Reporter*, March 21, 2008.

Heidi Schlumpf "Owning Unearned White Privilege," *National Catholic Reporter*, May 26, 2006.

Mary Ellen Schoonmaker "Bias Doesn't Always Need a Baseball Bat," *Bergen County (NJ) Record*, June 15, 2006.

Connie Schultz "The Right Approach to Confronting Racism," *New Jersey Star-Ledger*, October 7, 2008.

Earl Shorris "A Nation of WASPs?" *Nation*, May 31, 2004.

Gene Smith

"America Learned Racism; It Can Unlearn It, Too," *Fayetteville (NC) Observer*, October 6, 2007.

Brent Staples

"Barack Obama, John McCain, and the Language of Race," *New York Times*, September 22, 2008.

Shelby Steele

"The Age of White Guilt," *Toronto Globe & Mail*, October 25, 2007.

Andrew Stephen

"The Latino Giant Awakes," *New Statesman*, May 1, 2006.

William Storey

"Race and Ethnicity in U.S. Politics," *Politics Review*, September 2007.

Stuart Taylor Jr.

"The Great Black-White Hope," *Atlantic Monthly*, February 6, 2007.

Cynthia Tucker

"Racism Pales in Comparison to Thug Culture," *Atlanta Journal Constitution*, January 15, 2006.

Tara Wall

"Rhetorical Racism: The Futility of Polling Prejudice This Election," *Washington Times*, September 23, 2008.

Armstrong Williams

"Should Black People Let Affirmative Action Die? Yes," *Ebony*, January 2008.

Robert L. Woodson Sr.

"Obama and a Post-racial America," *Washington Times*, April 12, 2008.

Index